Ghosts

HENRIK IBSEN

Miss Julia

AUGUST STRINDBERG

Crofts Classics

GENERAL EDITOR

Samuel H. Beer, *Harvard University*

HENRIK IBSEN

Ghosts

A Family Drama in Three Acts

and

AUGUST STRINDBERG

Miss Julia

A Naturalistic Tragedy

translated and edited by
Thaddeus L. Torp
Central Connecticut State University

Harlan Davidson, Inc.
Arlington Heights, Illinois 60004

Library of Congress Cataloging-in-Publication Data

Ibsen, Henrik, 1828–1906.
    [Gengangere. English]
    Ghosts : a family drama in three acts / Henrik Ibsen. And
Miss Julia : a naturalistic tragedy / August Strindberg ; trans-
lated and edited by Thaddeus L. Torp.
        p.   cm. — (Crofts classics)
    Tranlation of: Gengangere / Henrik Ibsen; and Miss Julia
/ August Strindberg.
Includes bibliographical references (p. 117).
    ISBN 0-88295-128-9
    I. Torp, Thaddeus L.   II. Strindberg, August, 1849–1912.
Fröken Julie. English.   1992.   III. Title.
PT8865.A38   1992
839.8′226—dc20   91-25964
                                                                    CIP

Manufactured in the United States of America

96 95 94 93 92 1 2 3 4 5   MG

With Love and Appreciation
to Klemet & Anne

contents

introduction

The two plays in this small volume hold a prominent and unique position in each of the major countries of Europe where the "independent" or "free" theatre movement developed at the end of the nineteenth century. They thus have contributed to the development of twentieth-century dramatic writing and serve as a major link to contemporary methods of performance. Both works have come to be looked upon as watershed events in the critical response to what we now accept as the Modern Drama.

In most of Europe in the nineteenth century, plays could not be performed for public audiences until they had been approved by a censor and accepted by one of the few national playhouses which held monopolistic licenses. Critical response to *Ghosts* on its publication in December of 1881 was so universally damning that public performance was unthinkable by any reputable theatre. Indeed, the printed edition was returned to the publisher by most booksellers, and it was regarded as a volume not to be seen in respectable hands or homes. But the widespread following developed by the printed text indicated a waiting, if not universal, audience for this play and the others that were soon being written in the realistic and naturalistic mode. André Antoine, a clerk for the Paris Gas Company with little theatre experience but a great enthusiasm for Ibsen and his French followers, came up with a solution to this dilemma that was to result in a worldwide movement for "independent" or "free" theatre.

Antoine's concept was to run a theatre by subscription, a private organization open only to members. This permitted presentation of uncensored works which otherwise would have been denied licensing under the strict government standards in France. Performance would be in a small rented space on days when the regular bill was not being performed. This type of theatre eventually developed a following and function much like the present-day practice of Off-Off Broadway in which professional actors showcase new playwrights' work on their day off.

The opening of Antoine's groundbreaking Théâtre Libre (the Free Theatre) in Paris in 1887 demonstrated a legal and viable venue for the new drama, and its success inspired many imitators. One of the first non-French works performed by Antoine was Ibsen's *Ghosts,* which set off a widely publicized debate in the French Senate calling for new and stricter censorship for theatre.

The success of Antoine's venture and the publicity it engendered had a strong impact throughout the continent. Strindberg attempted to set up a theatre similar to Antoine's theatre in Copenhagen in 1887 with no success, but he did write a number of short one-act plays which he felt suitable for the new theatre: these of course included *Miss Julia.* But publication of *Miss Julia* met the same kind of press *Ghosts* had earlier elicited, and it had to be withdrawn from production.

The experimental productions worked under more experienced hands when Die Freie Bühne (the Free Theatre) under the direction of Otto Brahm opened in Berlin with a production of *Ghosts* in 1889. Brahm, a drama critic, had deliberately selected Ibsen's play as his opening salvo to clear the way for the new art while simultaneously heralding the radical tone his theatre hoped to establish. As in Antoine's case, Die Freie Bühne's subsequent season featured plays by Zola, Tolstoy, and Strindberg (*Miss Julia* as well as *The Father*). The theatre also established new German playwrights, most notably Gerhart Hauptmann.

England did not wait long to follow the Continental example. On March 13, 1891, the aptly named Independent Theatre also opened with a production of *Ghosts.* Chosen deliberately by the group's founder, J. T. Grein, who regarded Ibsen as the champion of the new drama of literary and artistic rather than commercial value, the production produced a vituperative storm in the press, of an intensity that we find difficult to comprehend today. The publicity thus engendered for the group was of course invaluable, and almost overnight Ibsen became a name known to every English newspaper reader. A theatrical interest had become a serious literary concern. It was into this foray that George Bernard Shaw determined to throw his considerable talents when he forsook criticism to write plays for production with the fledgling group.

In addition to the organizational similarities, each of these Independent Theatres also shared and therefore passed on to our contemporary practice certain production methods and philosophies. Antoine had been concerned with realism in staging from the very beginning, and the concise, conversational style of Ibsen, along with the acoustics of the small theatres demanded that grand theatrical delivery be abandoned. The new closeness of audience to stage and the ever-present subtext discovered in a close study of the scripts combined with a growing psychological awareness made subtlety of gesture and stage business a necessity. An entirely new, "modern" acting style had to be developed.

The small houses and compact demands of the scripts also made the box set a practical element of staging rather than the wing and drop sets in standard use at this time. Since properties and furniture were borrowed for each production, often from the homes of the producer's relatives, elements of naturalistic staging became expected adjuncts to the reality of the production. Advances in lighting kept pace, allowing Strindberg in his preface to *Miss Julia* to demand the removal of footlights with their "unnatural" effect and to call for more realistic application of makeup.

Antoine's first productions with the Théâtre Libre had been one-act plays. And the new theatres seemed to follow the course of shortening the time span of an evening's theatrical experience. Ibsen had already begun tightening the strictures of the full-length play to *Ghosts'* terse two and one-quarter hours. Strindberg proudly announced that in *Miss Julia* he had trimmed the tragedy down to its "meat" as the Greeks had done, to a single act of ninety minutes or less. The success of this experimental theatre movement attracted growing audiences who attended naturally evolving imitations throughout the western world, thus shaping public expectancy up to the present day: an audience view of the dynamics of the theatre to which both *Ghosts* and *Miss Julia* have made seminal contributions.

a note on Ibsen's ghostly humor

Laughter from the audience during the production of an Ibsen tragedy? Intermittent and appreciative laughter was building up during the performance of a "classic" drama by Norway's great playwright in the National Theatre in Oslo. There was no mistaking the reaction. This may have been my first visit to Norway, but laughter is the same in any language. A glance at the program reassured me: it was *Gengangere (Ghosts)* I was attending. On the stage stood Mrs. Alving's dowdy and somber parlor. Pastor Manders was launching into his reprimand of her lifestyle replete with high sounding biblical verbiage.

I turned to my Norwegian cousin, who was acting as my guide and translator on this my first visit to my father's native country. "Why are they laughing at him? Isn't this a serious discussion?" Shaw's fiery mandate flashed before my mind.

"Of course it is!" he whispered. "But we recognize that Manders is only *skin-holy.* That is why we laugh at what he says!"

"*Skin-holy.*" This peculiarly Norwegian expression for Mander's character trait enveloped the flow of dialogue that followed. I began to experience in the Norwegian-language production an insight that reading the play in English had never granted me.

Of course I was familiar at that time only with the Archer translations with their dated and curious British Victorianisms of speech. The only humor in these seemed to be the unconsciously mannered speech patterns imposed by the translator. Then more recently had come the angry Arthur Miller rewrite of *An Enemy of the People.* Praised for its stageworthiness, it has since been so widely anthologized that most theatre students think it to be representative Ibsen, altered ending and all! I have since discovered that all traces of comedy had been eradicated by the adaptor in his zealous pursuit of the tragic central theme.

I had been present in audiences provoked to laughter by clumsily mounted or overacted productions of nine-teenth-century plays. However, this Norwegian cast played and spoke naturally, no unnecessary histrionics, no farcical or melodramatic indulgence. This audience laughed at the by-play of character, and at what they re-alized to be going on beneath the "skin" (if you will) of the characters involved.

After that night in the theatre I made up my mind to rediscover the sense of humor in the grand old man of modern theatre; and to help clarify it to others, like myself, who had not been allowed to see this side of his creative nature before. But it was essential first to return to the original texts and start a new reading of each line. I hope that the following translation has been able to do that for my reader: to set forth clearly Henrik Ibsen's objective use of language so as to reveal the humor present in his view of character and character dialogue.

Another clue to his intended audience reaction came to me during my preparation of *When We Dead Awaken* for publication. In this, Ibsen's last play, the central character is Arnold Rubek, an aging artist, who is regarded by most critics to be among Ibsen's most transparently autobio-graphical representations. Early in the play the old man muses aloud to his young wife concerning the sculptured likenesses which he has devoted a major share of his life to producing not because of the call of art but in order to collect the extravagant commission they bring.

RUBEK *(a slow smile)* Those are not exactly por-trait busts I have lowered myself to doing, Maia. . . . they are not really *portrait* busts, I tell you.

MAIA What are they then?

RUBEK Something lies covered over, something shadowy far within and far back of the busts—some-thing private which none of the people can see—. . . . *(Conclusively)* Only I can see it. And that amuses me to the heart.[1]

[1]Ibsen, Henrik, *When We Dead Awaken*, ed. and trans. Thaddeus L. Torp. (Arlington Heights: Harlan Davidson, Inc., 1977), Act I, 42–3.

So there is to be found beneath the skin of each characterization another level which the author felt his public did not see. And that was amusing to him. A modern audience that catches glimpses of these shadow presences in the language can feel the same sense of amusement. What comes across clearly in a first-rate production is the playwright's ability to observe and objectify, to be amused even where he should be most angry.

Take the example of Manders, whom many regard to be a particularly strong target of Ibsen's wrath. The character may sound virulently selfrighteous, armed with dangerously pious moral indignation as he is. But we soon come to see him laughingly, as does Mrs. Alving, as a "great big child" who somehow only deserves a hug not punishment. Ibsen has filled his speeches with florid and fleeting linguistic references to the Old Testament language. It is a mannerism still adopted by fundamentalist preachers.

Engstrand (the character who comes close to melodramatic villainy complete with a club-footed limp) is likewise treated humorously, mimicking this pretentious speech pattern whenever he seeks favor from the man of the cloth. However, to our amusement he readily lapses into bad grammar and swearing when provoked by Regina. Regina's speech is also satirically controlled. She uses French phrases pretentiously, and then assures the old carpenter it is "English." The language patterns of these characters are worked out, it would seem, to emphasize their comic aspects and their inner motivations.

Michael Meyers's thorough biography has the following to say of Ibsen's contribution to the language of the stage in the present century:

> [Ibsen] developed the art of prose dialogue to a degree of refinement which has never been surpassed; not merely the different ways people talk, and the different language they use under differing circumstances, but that double-density dialogue which is his peculiar legacy, the sub text, the meaning behind the meaning.[2]

[2]Meyer, Michael. *Ibsen: A Biography* (Penguin Books, 1985), 862.

Subtext, while it can supply humor (Engstrand's explanation for his injured leg is an amusing example), can also
prevent a mildly amusing situation from being outright
comic in the eyes of an audience. The dramatic irony of
the money that Manders has so scrupulously and religiously
invested going at last to a home for wayward seamen, and
even Regina's melodramatic exit to work in "Chamberlain
Alving's Home," causes a wry smile of humor, but the
weight of its tragic impact on Mrs. Alving represses any
laughter. Even the feeble, but overtly comic outcry of Manders that caps Act II: "And it isn't insured!" becomes in
contrast a starkly tragic lament as the curtain falls in silence. Humorous response is as carefully controlled in this
great play as the symbolic and structural elements.

notes on the translation

The first difficulty facing a translator of these two plays, I
feel, is the problem set forth by their titles; each bears a
word whose connotative value in English gives a somewhat
incorrect slant to the content of the play as it is perceived
on first reading. However, both plays have also been known
so universally by their respective titles that the new translator tampers with the word choice at his peril.

Ghosts is the standard English translation of the play
Ibsen called *Gengangere*. The Norwegian word does not
refer to the spirits or souls of dead people. That would
require the word "Spök," as in the title of Strindberg's
Ghost Sonata. "Gengangere" refers to things and ideas that
return to haunt the living. *Hauntings*, however, would give
the play an undue mystery-thriller sound. And *Ghosts* is
so universally well known a translation that it must remain.

Miss Julia comes from Strindberg's *Fröken Julie*. "Fröken" is a title of nobility as well as a designation of unmarried status. Although the play concerns itself very
much with social class distinctions, the designation "Lady"
does not quite fill the bill and tends to remove the play
too much from its popular notoriety. "Julie," however, as

it appears in most translations, leads us to mispronounce the main character's name. I have therefore opted for "Julia" which retains Strindberg's rhythm and gives her, I think, more elegance.

Within *Miss Julia* problems occur when Jean refers to Julia as his "mistress," a word which in our time has another meaning. The terms of addressing an individual pose a different problem in *Ghosts*, as Manders is sometimes referred to as pastor or priest (the title for his profession) and other times is addressed as "Herr Pastor," a very formal designation similar to "Your Reverence." I have retained "pastor" or "the pastor" where his position is referred to and used the common protestant title "Reverend" when formality is needed ("Reverend, Sir," when characters address him directly).

As in my previous translations, I have taken particular care to accurately convey the set description and stage directions of the author. Ibsen was, after all, an experienced stage director and noted for the succinct nature of his critical comments to actors and technical aids. Strindberg prepared and wrote *Miss Julia* especially for his Experimental Theatre in Copenhagen; so the reader will note that some of the stage directions are intended more to aid production than to help the reader visualize the drama.

chronology of important

Ibsen

events and principal works

Strindberg

1849	Born: Stockholm, Sweden, January 22
1862	Death of his mother
1867	Student at Uppsala University
1869	Student at Royal Academy of Acting
1870	First published play: *The Free Thinker*; *In Rome* performed at Royal Theatre
1877	Marriage to Siri von Essen
1879	*The Red Room* (a novel): first literary success
1881	*Master Olof*: successful in performance
1882	*Lucky Per's Journey*
1883	Leaves Scandinavia
1884	The play *Married*; unsuccessfully prosecuted for blasphemy
1886	Autobiography (four volumes)
1887	*The Father*; *Comrades*; plans for an Experimental Theatre in Denmark

1888	*The Lady from the Sea*
1889	Die Freie Bühne opens with *Ghosts*
1890	*Hedda Gabler*; Antoine stages *Ghosts*
1891	Returns to Oslo, Norway; *Ghosts* in England at Independant Theatre
1892	*The Master Builder*
1894	*Little Eyolf*
1896	*John Gabriel Borkman*
1898	No play; 70th birthday caused celebrations and revivals
1899	*When We Dead Awaken*: the last play
1900	Deteriorating health
1901	Paralyzed by a stroke
1906	Died May 23, Oslo, Norway

1888	*Miss Julia*; published to negative review. Attempted to establish an Independant Theatre in Copenhagen
1891	Divorced Siri
1892	*The Bond*; *Motherlove*; *Playing with Fire*
1893	Marriage to Frida Uhl
1894	Separated; beginning of *Inferno* crisis
1896	Return to Sweden at Lund
1897	*Inferno*; Divorce from Frida
1898	*To Damascus I & II*; copy sent to Ibsen
1899	*Crimes and Crimes*; *Gustav Vasa*; and historical plays; return to Stockholm
1900	*Dance of Death*; *Easter*; a greatly productive year
1901	Married to Harriet Bosse; *Swanwhite*; *Queen Christina*; *To Damascus III*
1902	Separated; *A Dream Play*; *Gustav III*
1904	Divorced Harriet
1906	Historical prose; last volume of autobiography
1907	Founded Intimate Theatre; wrote the Chamber Plays (incl. *Ghost Sonata*)
1909	*The Great Highway*; the last play
1912	Died May 14 of cancer in Stockholm

Neither author received the Nobel Prize. For events and dates, I am primarily indebted to F. L. Lucas, *The Drama of Ibsen and Strindberg*, 1962.

Ghosts

A Family Drama in Three Acts

HENRIK IBSEN

1881

Translated from the Norwegian by

Thaddeus L. Torp

Characters

MRS. HELENA ALVING, *widow of* CAPTAIN ALVING *who had been by appointment chamberlain to the king*
OSWALD ALVING, *her son, an artist*
PASTOR MANDERS
JACOB ENGSTRAND, *a carpenter*
REGINA ENGSTRAND, *a household servant of* MRS. ALVING

(The action takes place at MRS. ALVING'S *country estate on one of the large fjords in western Norway.)*

Act One

(A roomy parlor with one door on the left side and two doors to the right. In the middle of the room is a round table with chairs around it; on the table are books, magazines, and newspapers. Downstage left is a window in front of which is a small sofa and a sewing table. Upstage the room opens into a somewhat narrower sun porch or plant room completely enclosed with large-paned glass windows. In the right wall of this sun porch is a door which leads down to the garden. Through the glass wall can be seen the gloomy slopes of the fjord veiled by a steady drizzling rain.

ENGSTRAND, *the carpenter, is standing by the garden door. His left leg is slightly deformed and he has a thick piece of wood attached to that boot sole.* REGINA, *with an empty watering can in her hand, is trying to prevent him from coming in.)*

REGINA. *(In a low voice)* What do you want? Stay where you are! You're dripping all over!

ENGSTRAND. It's the Lord's rain it is, my child. *paternal*

REGINA. That's the devil's rain, that is.

ENGSTRAND. Geez, how you talk, Regina. *(He limps a few steps into the room.)* But I only came here to say that—

REGINA. Don't clomp so with that foot, man! The young master is sleeping upstairs.

ENGSTRAND. He's still in bed? At this hour of the day?

REGINA. That's none of your business.

ENGSTRAND. I was out drinking last night—

REGINA. I believe that.

ENGSTRAND. Yah, all men have their weaknesses, my child—

REGINA. That's true enough.

ENGSTRAND. —and the temptations of this world are manifold, you see—; but in spite of all that, by God, I was back at work by five thirty this morning.

REGINA. Yes, yes, well clear out now. I'm not going to stand here and have a *rendez-vous* with you. *French*

ENGSTRAND. You're not *what*?

REGINA. I don't want anyone to see you in here. So get along now!

ENGSTRAND. By God, I'm not going till I've had a chance to talk to you. This afternoon I'll be through with the work down there at the schoolhouse, and I'll be going back over to town on the boat tonight.

REGINA. *(Mumbling)* Pleasant journey!

ENGSTRAND. Thanks for that, my child. Tomorrow they dedicate the orphanage, you see, and it's going to be a fancy affair with lots of alcohol. And I don't want anyone to say that Jacob Engstrand can't resist that sort of temptation.

REGINA. Aha!

ENGSTRAND. Yah, well, there'll be a lot of high-class folks attending this thing tomorrow. Pastor Manders himself is expected from town.

REGINA. He's coming out today.

ENGSTRAND. Is that so? Well I'll be damned if I'll give him anything to say about me.

REGINA. Aha! So that's what you're up to?

ENGSTRAND. What do you mean "up to"?

REGINA. *(Looking knowingly at him)* What sort of trick are you trying to put over on Pastor Manders this time?

ENGSTRAND. Such a crazy thing to say! Me trying to trick Pastor Manders? Oh, no, the pastor is too good a friend for me to do *that*. But I have to talk to you now, you see, because I'm going back home tonight.

REGINA. You're not going too soon for me.

ENGSTRAND. Yes, but I'm taking you with me, Regina.

REGINA. *(Her mouth falls open in disbelief.)* You're taking me—? What did you say?

ENGSTRAND. I said: "I'm taking you home with me!"

REGINA. *(Scornfully)* You'll never, ever get me to go to your home.

ENGSTRAND. Oh, we'll see about that.

REGINA. Yes. You can bet we'll see. *I*, who was brought up in this house, the house of a great lady like Mrs. Alving—? *I* who was treated almost like her own child—? Could *I* move home with *you*? To such a place? Pooh!

ENGSTRAND. What the hell? Are you setting yourself up against your own father, you tramp?

REGINA. *(Mumbling without looking at him)* You often said I was not your concern.

ENGSTRAND. —Aw, well, let's forget that—

REGINA. What about all the times you scolded me and called me a—? *"Fi donc!"*

ENGSTRAND. God help me, I never used such an awful word!

REGINA. Oh, I know well enough the word you used.

ENGSTRAND. Yah, well, that was when your mother was acting uppity. I had to find a way to teach her her place. She was always one to put on airs. *(Mimicking)* "Let go of me, Engstrand! Let me be! I was in service for three years with Chamberlain Alving at Rose Manor!" *(Laughing)* Jesus; always had to remind us that the captain became a chamberlain while she worked here.

REGINA. Poor Mother;—Your bullying killed her!

ENGSTRAND. *(Turning away)* Sure, sure! I'm guilty of everything.

REGINA. *(Also turning, mutters under breath)* Ooof—! And that leg.

ENGSTRAND. What did you say, girl?

REGINA. *Pied de mouton.* foot of sheep

ENGSTRAND. Is that English, that?

REGINA. Yes.

ENGSTRAND. Sure, sure: you've gotten some educating out here, and that can come in handy now, it can, Regina.

REGINA. *(After a short silence)* Just what is it you want me for in town?

ENGSTRAND. Can you beat that, asking what a father wants of his only child? Ain't I a lonely, forsaken widower?

REGINA. Oh, don't give me that. What do you want me back there for?

ENGSTRAND. Well, I'll tell you. I've been thinking about starting in on something new now.

REGINA. *(Disgustedly)* You've done that before. What good did it do you?

ENGSTRAND. This time'll be different, Regina! —I'll be damned if—

REGINA. *(Stamping her foot)* Don't swear!

ENGSTRAND. Hush, hush; you're right, child! I just want to say I've put up quite a little bit of money from my work here on this new orphan-asylum.

REGINA. Have you? Well, good for you.

ENGSTRAND. What was there to spend it on out here in the sticks?

REGINA. Well, so?

ENGSTRAND. So, you see, I've been thinking of using this money for something that will make me a profit. I've been thinking of a sort of public house for sailors—

REGINA. Ugh!

ENGSTRAND. A real high-class place, you understand —not just your common flop-house for the crew. No, by God—it would be for ships' captains and officers and—and really high-class folks, you understand.

REGINA. And I'm supposed to—?

ENGSTRAND. You'll help out, you see. Only for the sake of appearances, you know what I mean. You won't have to work very damn hard, child. You can arrange it any way you like.

REGINA. Oh, sure!

ENGSTRAND. Well, there's got to be a woman in the house, that's clear enough. Because in the evenings we've got to have a little fun, with singing and dancing and stuff like that. You must remember these seamen are wanderers adrift on life's great ocean. *(Coming closer)* Now you'd be stupid to miss this chance, Regina. What can you do for yourself out here? What good does it do you, this here expensive education Mrs. Alving has given you? You're supposed to care for the kids in the new orphanage, I hear. Is that for the likes of you? Are you going to destroy your health working for so many grubby brats?

REGINA. Not if I get my way, then,—well, it's possible. It *is* possible!

ENGSTRAND. What is?

REGINA. Nothing to worry your head about.—Is it a lot of money, that you've saved out here?

ENGSTRAND. Somewhere between seven—eight hundred crowns!

REGINA. That's not bad.

ENGSTRAND. It's a start.

REGINA. And you're not going to give me any of that?

ENGSTRAND. Not a chance in Hell!

REGINA. Not even enough so I can make myself a new dress?

ENGSTRAND. Just come to town with me, and you'll have dresses enough.

REGINA. Pooh! I could do that on my own if I wanted to.

ENGSTRAND. No, Regina, it's better to have a father's protecting hand. I have my eye on a house on Little Harbor Street. They don't want much for it; and there we could set up a sort of sailor's hostelry, you see.

REGINA. But I *will not* live with *you*! I don't want anything to do with you. So, get out!

ENGSTRAND. You wouldn't be living very long with me, my girl. Damn the luck! If you know how to play the game. You're a pretty wench and you've really filled out this year—

REGINA. Well—?

ENGSTRAND. It wouldn't be long before a ship's officer,— sure, even—a captain maybe—

REGINA. I will not marry any of them. Sailors have no *savoir vivre.* Knowledge of living

ENGSTRAND. Haven't got no what?

REGINA. I know sailors, I said. They're not the kind I want to marry.

ENGSTRAND. So don't marry 'em then. There's money enough without that. *(Confidentially)* Him—the English-man—the one with the yacht—he came across with three hundred dollars cash, he did;—and she wasn't any prettier than you.

REGINA. *(Goes toward him)* Get out, you!

ENGSTRAND. *(Cowers)* Now, now, you wouldn't hit me, would you?

REGINA. Yes! Say one more word about my mother and I will! Get out, I tell you! *(Driving him back to the garden door)* And don't slam the door; the young Mister Alving—

ENGSTRAND. I know, he's sleeping. It's strange you worry so much about the young Mister Alving—*(Softly)* Aha; You wouldn't by any chance be thinking that *he*—?

REGINA. Out, and be quick! You're crazy! No, not that way. Here comes Pastor Manders. Go down the kitchen stairs.

ENGSTRAND. *(Going right)* Yes, yes, I'll go. But you ask that man there. He'll remind you of a child's duty to her father. For I am your father no matter what you say. I can prove it by the church registry, I can. *(He exits by the far door which Regina opens and then closes after him.)*

*(*REGINA *examines herself hastily in a mirror, fans her-self with a handkerchief and adjusts her collar; then she begins to fuss with the flowers and plants.*

PASTOR MANDERS *enters through the garden door and comes into the plant room. He is wearing an overcoat and carrying an umbrella, and he has a small travelling case on a strap over his shoulder.)*

MANDERS.   Good morning, Miss Engstrand.

REGINA.   *(Turning with a pleased and surprised expression)* Why, good morning, Reverend! Has the boat come already?

MANDERS.   Just in. *(Going to the parlor)* It's tiresome, this steady rain we're having today.

REGINA.   *(Following him)* It's a good sign for farmers, Reverend.

MANDERS.   Yes, you're right there. We city folks forget about that. *(Beginning to take off his coat)*

REGINA.   Oh, let me help!—There. Oh, it's all wet! I'd better hang it up in the hall. And the umbrella—; I'll open it up and let it dry. *(She takes the things out the Up-Right door,* PASTOR MANDERS *sets his briefcase and hat on a chair.* REGINA *returns immediately.)*

MANDERS.   Oh, it's good to be indoors again. Well, I trust everything is going well here at Rose Manor?

REGINA.   Yes, thank you.

MANDERS.   You're busy, I suppose, preparing for tomorrow?

REGINA.   Oh yes, there's quite a bit to be done.

MANDERS.   Mrs. Alving is at home, I assume?

REGINA.   Of course; she's just gone upstairs with hot chocolate for the young master.

MANDERS.   Oh, yes, I heard at the dock that Oswald had arrived.

REGINA.   Yes, he came yesterday. We didn't expect him until today.

MANDERS.   How is he, healthy, and in good spirits?

REGINA.   Yes, thanks, I think so. But very tired after the trip. He came straight through nonstop from Paris—; I mean he didn't even change trains. I think he's taking a nap now, so we'd better not talk very loud.

MANDERS.   Shhh! We'll be very quiet.

REGINA. *(Arranging an easy chair next to the table)* Please sit here, Reverend, Sir, and make yourself comfortable. *(He sits; she puts a footstool under his feet.)* There! Now isn't that nice?

MANDERS. Thank you; that's very comfortable. *(Looking her over)* You know, Miss Engstrand, you've really grown up since I last saw you.

REGINA. Do you think so, sir? Mrs. Alving says I have filled out also.

MANDERS. Filled out? Oh, well, a little;—not too much. *(Short pause)*

REGINA. Should I let madam know you're here?

MANDERS. Thank you, there's no hurry, dear child.— Well, then, tell me, Regina, how is your father getting along out here?

REGINA. He's doing alright, thank you, Reverend.

MANDERS. He came to see me the last time he was in town.

REGINA. Oh, did he? He's always glad to have a chance to speak to you, sir.

MANDERS. And I suppose you go down and see him every day.

REGINA. Me? Oh, yes, of course; whenever I find the time—

MANDERS. Your father doesn't have a very strong will-power, Miss Engstrand. He's much in need of a guiding hand.

REGINA. Oh yes, I know that.

MANDERS. He needs to have someone nearby to show him a little affection, and whose opinions he can look up to. He openly admitted that himself, the last time he visited me.

REGINA. Yes, he said something like that to me, too. But I don't know whether Mrs. Alving would let me go—especially now, with the new orphanage to run. Besides, I'd be sad to leave Mrs. Alving. She's always been so good to me.

MANDERS. But, dear girl, a daughter's duty—Naturally we will first get Mrs. Alving's consent.

REGINA. But I don't think, at my age, it would be proper to keep house for an unmarried man.

MANDERS. What! But my dear Miss Engstrand, this is your own father we're talking about!

REGINA. Yes, but all the same—. Oh, if it were a really *nice* house and he were a real gentleman—

MANDERS. But, my dear Regina—

REGINA. —Someone I could respect and look up to and really be a daughter to—

MANDERS. Yes, but my good child—

REGINA. Then I wouldn't mind going back to town. It does get lonely out here,—and you yourself know, sir, what it's like to be alone in the world. And I don't mind saying I'm clever and willing. Perhaps the pastor knows of a position of that sort for me?

MANDERS. I? No, I'm afraid I don't.

REGINA. But dear sir, dear Pastor—please remember me if one comes up—

MANDERS. *(Standing up)* Yes, I certainly will, Miss Engstrand.

REGINA. Yes, because if I—

MANDERS. Please inform Mrs. Alving that I am here.

REGINA. She will be right down, sir. *(She exits left.)*

MANDERS. *(Walks up and down the room a couple of times; stands for a while upstage and looks out into the garden with his hands behind his back. Then he walks back to the table, takes up a book and looks at the title; startled, he examines others.)* Hmm,—so!

(MRS. ALVING comes through the door stage left. She is followed by REGINA, who immediately goes out by the door down right.)

MRS. ALVING. *(Holding out her hand)* Welcome to Rose Manor, Pastor.

MANDERS. Good morning, Mrs. Alving. Here I am as I promised.

MRS. ALVING. Always so punctual.

MANDERS. But you know it wasn't easy for me to get away. All these blessed committees and boards I sit on—

MRS. ALVING. All the kinder of you to come, and to come early. Now we can go over the business before dinner. But where's your luggage?

MANDERS. *(Quickly)* My things are down at the hotel. I'll be staying there.

MRS. ALVING. *(Covering a smile)* You mean I can't persuade you to stay overnight in my house even now?

MANDERS. No, no, Mrs. Alving—thanks all the same; I'll sleep down there as usual. It's so convenient for boarding the boat.

MRS. ALVING. Well, do what you will, but I really think that we two old folks—

MANDERS. Good heavens, now you're joking. Yes, it's only natural you feel jolly today. With the celebration tomorrow and having Oswald home.

MRS. ALVING. Yes, you can imagine how wonderful that is for me! It's over two years since he was last home. And he's promised to stay all winter.

MANDERS. No, has he? How like a good son that is. I can well imagine there are many more attractive reasons to live in Rome or Paris.

MRS. ALVING. Yes, but his home is here with his mother, you see. The affection he continues to show me is a blessing.

MANDERS. It would be sad indeed if distance from you and such things as his art were able to dull that natural feeling.

MRS. ALVING. Yes, but there's no danger of that happening to my boy. It'll amuse me to see if you recognize him. He'll be down later; he's just resting a little on the sofa up there—But please do sit down, my dear Pastor.

MANDERS. Thank you. You're certain this is convenient—?

MRS. ALVING. Of course it is. *(She sits by the table.)*

MANDERS. Good. Then first let's see—*(Going to the chair where he put his briefcase, he takes a packet of papers out of it, seats himself at the opposite side of the table and searches for a place to put down the papers.)* Well to begin, here we have— *(Breaking off)* Tell me, Mrs. Alving, what are *these* books doing *here*?

MRS. ALVING. These books? I've been reading them.

MANDERS. You actually read this sort of thing?

MRS. ALVING. Of course I do.

MANDERS. Does reading this kind of thing improve you or bring you pleasure?

MRS. ALVING. I find it gives me confidence.

MANDERS. How remarkable. In what way?

MRS. ALVING. Well, these books explain and confirm many of the ideas I've had myself. Yes, that is the surprising thing, Pastor Manders,—there really is nothing new in these books; not really anything in them that most men don't already think and believe. It's only that most people won't be honest with themselves and admit it.

MANDERS. But, dear Lord! Do you seriously believe that *most* people—?

MRS. ALVING. Yes, I certainly do.

MANDERS. But surely not in this country. Not our kind?

MRS. ALVING. Yes—just like us.

MANDERS. Well, I don't know what to say—!

MRS. ALVING. But what do you object to in these books?

MANDERS. Object? You don't really think I can spare the time to study such publications?

MRS. ALVING. In other words you have no idea of what you've been condemning.

MANDERS. I have read enough *about* these writings to disapprove of them.

MRS. ALVING. Yes, but your own opinion—

MANDERS. Dear woman, there are many occasions in life when one must rely on other men's opinions. That's how it is in this world, and it's just as well. How else could society survive?

MRS. ALVING. No, of course; you could be right there.

MANDERS. Of course I can't deny that there may be much that attracts you to these writings. And I can't blame you for wanting to read and know about these intellectual trends which one hears are going on in the outside world,—

where you have allowed your son to ramble for so long. However— *condemning*

MRS. ALVING. However—?

MANDERS. *(Lowering his voice)* However one doesn't talk about such things, Mrs. Alving. One should not be required to explain to everyone what one reads and thinks inside one's own four walls.

MRS. ALVING. Naturally not.

MANDERS. But remember you must always consider the orphanage, which was begun at a time when your thinking was quite different from what it seems to be now; as far as I can tell.

MRS. ALVING. I agree with you there. But it was about the orphanage—

MANDERS. Yes, yes, one final word—discretion, my dear! And now back to the business of the orphanage. *(Opening the packet, he takes out some of the papers.)* This is what you want to see.

MRS. ALVING. The deeds?

MANDERS. Everything. And all completed. As you can imagine it wasn't easy for me to get them all drawn up in time. I had to apply some pressure. The authorities are painfully conscientious when it comes to making decisions. But here they are, nonetheless. *(Leafing through the bundle)* See, here is the transfer of title for the Solvik farmstead in the aforesaid Rose Manor Estate, with all newly constructed buildings, dormitories, classrooms, teacherage, and chapel. And here is the settlement of endowment and trust fund for the institution. Look them over—*(Reading)* Deed of Trust for the Children's Home: "The Captain Alving Memorial."

MRS. ALVING. *(Staring for a long time at the paper)* So there it is.

MANDERS. I chose to say "captain" rather than "chamberlain." "captain" doesn't look so pretentious.

MRS. ALVING. Oh yes, whatever you think best.

MANDERS. And here I have the account book from the bank where the capital to cover the running expenses of the orphanage has been deposited.

MRS. ALVING. Thank you. But I would prefer that you keep that.

MANDERS. Very well. I think we should leave the money in the bank for the time being. Of course, the interest isn't very attractive; 4 percent and six months withdrawal notice. Later on we might come across a good mortgage,—of course it would have to be a first mortgage and absolutely guaranteed,—then we might consider it as an investment.

MRS. ALVING. Yes, yes, dear Pastor Manders, you know what is best.

MANDERS. I'll keep my eyes open.—But there's something else I've been meaning to ask you.

MRS. ALVING. And what is that?

MANDERS. Do you want insurance on the orphanage buildings or not?

MRS. ALVING. Naturally they should be insured.

MANDERS. Now wait a moment, Mrs. Alving. Let's give it closer consideration.

MRS. ALVING. Everything I own is insured: buildings, personal effects, crops and livestock.

MANDERS. Personal holdings. Those are your own property. The same with my own, naturally. But this, you see, is quite another thing. The orphanage is to be consecrated to a higher purpose.

MRS. ALVING. Yes, but—

MANDERS. For my own personal sake I don't see any harm in protecting ourselves against all possibilities.

MRS. ALVING. Nor do I.

MANDERS. —But what is the general feeling in the community? You can judge that better than I.

MRS. ALVING. The feeling—?

MANDERS. Are there any prominent people—whose opinions really matter—who might take offense?

MRS. ALVING. What do you mean: people whose opinions matter?

MANDERS. —Well, I'm thinking of the kind of people in such independent and influential positions that we can't very well ignore their opinions.

Mrs. Alving. There are some people here who might take offense—

Manders. There, you see! There are many like that in town. Think of my colleagues and their followers! People could easily come to the conclusion that neither you nor I have sufficient faith in higher power.

Mrs. Alving. But as far as you're concerned, my dear Pastor, surely you know deep inside that—

Manders. Oh, I know; I know;—My own conscience is clear on that, you may be sure. But we must also avoid any chance for wrong or unfavorable interpretation. Especially one that might have an adverse influence on the operation of the asylum.

Mrs. Alving. Well, if *that* is the case then—

Manders. I can hardly overlook the difficult—yes, even I might say, painful position *I* would find myself in. Among the best circles in town there is much interest in this orphanage. It is to be operated as a service to the town as well as the country-folk out here, and there is hope it will lighten the community poor-taxes. Since I have served as your financial advisor and managed the business affairs I very much fear that the zealous ones will direct their attacks against *me* if the expenses are—

Mrs. Alving. Yes, you must not leave yourself open to that.

Manders. To say nothing of the assault which would most certainly be launched against me in certain papers and periodicals which—

Mrs. Alving. Enough, my dear Pastor; then it's settled.

Manders. Then you do not wish to have the orphanage insured?

Mrs. Alving. No; we'll let it be.

Manders. *(Leaning back in the chair)* But *should* an accident take place? You never know—. Would you be able to cover the damages?

Mrs. Alving. No, I'll tell you right now I most certainly could not.

Manders. In that case, Mrs. Alving,—this responsibility we are taking on ourselves is very serious indeed.

MRS. ALVING. Then tell me what else *can* we do?

MANDERS. That's just the thing; there's nothing else we *can* do. We must not leave ourselves open to any misinterpretation; and we cannot afford to offend public opinion.

MRS. ALVING. Well certainly you can't, as a minister.

MANDERS. And I also firmly believe that we must have faith that such an institution will have good fortune on its side—. Yes, it will stand under a specially blessed protection.

MRS. ALVING. Let us hope so, Pastor Manders.

MANDERS. Shall we leave it at that?

MRS. ALVING. Yes, let's leave it.

MANDERS. Good. *As you wish. (Making a note)* Note—not-to-be-insured.

MRS. ALVING. By the way, it's odd that you mentioned this today.—

MANDERS. I've often thought of bringing it to your attention—.

MRS. ALVING. —because just yesterday we almost had a fire down there.

MANDERS. What!

MRS. ALVING. Well, it wasn't really anything, you see. Some shavings caught fire in the carpenter shop.

MANDERS. Where Engstrand works?

MRS. ALVING. Yes. He's often careless with matches, they say.

MANDERS. He has so many things on his mind, poor man. —all kinds of temptations. God be praised, he's making a real effort to live a decent life, I hear.

MRS. ALVING. Oh? Who said that?

MANDERS. He assured me of that himself. And he is also a good worker.

MRS. ALVING. Oh, yes. As long as he's sober—

MANDERS. Yes, that unfortunate weakness! But he is often forced to succumb to it because of his bad leg, he says. Last time he was in town I was really touched. He came to see me so cordially in order to thank me for finding him work out here so that he could be near Regina.

MRS. ALVING. I don't think he sees much of her.

MANDERS. Oh, yes, he talks with her every day; he told me that himself.

MRS. ALVING. Oh well, that could be.

MANDERS. He feels very strongly that he needs to have someone who can hold him in check when the temptations come along. That's what is so lovable about Jacob Engstrand, he comes to you so helplessly and accuses himself and confesses his weaknesses. The last time he came in to talk to me—Tell me, Mrs. Alving, if it were absolutely necessary and vital for him to have Regina with him again—

MRS. ALVING. *(Suddenly rising)* Regina!

MANDERS. —You must not set yourself against it.

MRS. ALVING. I most certainly will. And furthermore— Regina is to have a position at the orphanage.

MANDERS. But remember, he is her very own father—

MRS. ALVING. Oh, I know very well what sort of father he has been to her. As for going back to live with him, no, I never, ever will consent to that. *She stands up for Regina*

MANDERS. *(Rising)* But, my dear Mrs. Alving, you mustn't react so violently. It is sad to see how you misjudge this man Engstrand. You almost seem to be afraid—

MRS. ALVING. *(More quietly)* Pay no heed. I have taken Regina into my home and here she will stay. *(Listening)* Shhh, my dear Pastor Manders, let's not talk anymore about it. *(Her face lighting up happily)* Listen! That's Oswald on the stairs. Now we can concentrate our thoughts on *him*.

(OSWALD enters through the left door. He is wearing a light overcoat, has a hat in his hand, and is smoking a large meerschaum pipe.)

OSWALD. *(Standing a moment in the door)* Oh, forgive me—I thought you were in the study *(Coming in)* How do you do, Pastor.

MANDERS. *(Staring)* Oh—! It's remarkable—

MRS. ALVING. Yes, what do you think of *him*, Pastor Manders.

MANDERS. I think,—I think—No, but is it really—?

OSWALD. Yes, sir! It really is the prodigal son.

MANDERS. But my dear young friend—

OSWALD. Well then the son returned home.

MRS. ALVING. Oswald is referring to how opposed you were to his becoming a painter.

MANDERS. In the eye of Man, many a step taken in doubt may only later be revealed as—. *(Shaking his hand)* But, welcome home! Welcome, my dear Oswald—Oh, I trust I may call you by your Christian name?

OSWALD. Yes, what else?

MANDERS. Good. What I was going to say, my dear Oswald, was this:—You must not think that I condemn the entire artistic profession. Certainly there are many who manage to keep their inner selves untarnished.

OSWALD. I should hope so.

MRS. ALVING. *(Beaming happily)* I know of one who has managed to keep his inner-self and his outer-self untarnished. Just see for yourself, Pastor.

OSWALD. *(Moving away from her)* Yes, yes, Mother, let's drop it.

MANDERS. No doubt of that—. Also you have begun to make a name for yourself. The papers here often mention you and always favorably it seems. But I must say—I haven't read anything about you lately.

OSWALD. *(Upstage by the flowers)* I haven't done much painting lately.

MRS. ALVING. Even a painter needs to rest now and then.

MANDERS. I imagine so. And that's how you prepare yourself to undertake a great work of some sort.

OSWALD. Yes.—Mother, how soon will we be dining?

MRS. ALVING. Less than half an hour. He still has a good appetite, thank Heaven.

MANDERS. And a taste for tobacco, I see.

OSWALD. I found Father's pipe in the room upstairs, so—

MANDERS. Aha, that explains it!

MRS. ALVING. What?

MANDERS. When Oswald came through that door with the pipe in his mouth it was the same as seeing his father alive again.

OSWALD. No, really?

MRS. ALVING. Oh, how can you say that! Oswald takes after me.

MANDERS. Yes; but there is a firmness at the corners of the mouth, something about the lips, that reminds me so vividly of Alving—especially while he is smoking.

MRS. ALVING. Not at all. Oswald has more the mouth of a minister, I believe.

MANDERS. Oh, yes, yes; many of my colleagues have the same set of mouth.

MRS. ALVING. But put away the pipe, my dear; I don't want the room all smoked-up.

OSWALD. *(Doing so)* All right. I only wanted to try it. I smoked it once when I was a child.

MRS. ALVING. You did?

OSWALD. Yes, when I was very small. I remember I went upstairs to Father's room in the evening. He was very happy and joking.

MRS. ALVING. Oh, you can't remember anything from those years.

OSWALD. Oh yes, I remember clearly. He picked me up and set me on his knee and made me smoke his pipe. "Smoke, boy" he said,—"Puff hard, boy!" And I puffed as hard as I could until I began to get sick and drops of sweat broke out on my forehead. And that made him shake with laughter—

MANDERS. What a strange thing to do.

MRS. ALVING. Heavens, it's only something Oswald has dreamed up.

OSWALD. No, Mother, I didn't just dream this up. Because—don't you remember, you came and carried me to the nursery. Then I got real sick, and you were crying. Did Father often play tricks like that?

MANDERS. As a young man he was always full of fun.—

OSWALD. And yet he accomplished so much in the world. So many good and useful things even though he didn't live long.

MANDERS. Yes, it is the name of an industrious and worthy man which you have inherited, my dear Oswald Alving. And it should serve to spur you on—

OSWALD. Yes, it should.

MANDERS. It was certainly good of you to come home and honor him on this special day.

OSWALD. It was the least I could do for my father.

MRS. ALVING. And I get to keep him for a while. That is by far the best part.

MANDERS. Yes, I hear that you plan to stay home through the winter.

OSWALD. I don't know how long I will be here, sir. —Oh, but it's great to be home!

MRS. ALVING. *(Beaming)* Yes, isn't it, dear?

MANDERS. *(Looking at him with sympathy)* You went out into the world so early, my dear Oswald.

OSWALD. That I did. I sometimes wonder if it wasn't *too* early.

MRS. ALVING. Nonsense. It's the best way for a boy to build character. It's bad for an only child to stay at home, his parents will spoil him.

MANDERS. That is a questionable theory, Mrs. Alving. The parental home is the child's rightful environment.

OSWALD. I agree with the pastor there.

MANDERS. Just take your own son, now. Yes, we might as well say it to his face. What price has he paid? He's reached the age of twenty-six or seven and has never had the opportunity to experience real home-life.

OSWALD. Pardon me, sir—but that is not true.

MANDERS. Oh? It was my understanding that you have spent all your time in artistic circles.

OSWALD. I have.

MANDERS. And mostly the younger artists.

OSWALD. Of course.

MANDERS. But I understand most of those folks are too poor to establish a family and support a home.

OSWALD. Many of them can't afford to marry, Pastor.

MRS. ALVING. Yes, that's what I meant.

OSWALD. But they still can have a home. And some of them do, and very nice, comfortable homes at that.

MRS. ALVING. *(Following what they say, nodding)*

MANDERS. I don't mean a bachelor's place. When I say home I mean a family household where a man lives with his wife and his children.

OSWALD. Yes; with his children and with their mother.

MANDERS. *(Startled; claps his hands)* But you don't mean—!

OSWALD. Well?

MANDERS. Living together with—the children's mother!

OSWALD. Yes, would you rather have him disown the mother of his children?

MANDERS. You are speaking of unlawful unions! These so-called "free marriages."

OSWALD. I don't see anything particularly "free" about the way these people live.

MANDERS. But how could it be possible for—a reasonably well-brought-up young man or woman to allow themselves to live like—right in front of everyone.

OSWALD. But what should they do? A poor young artist— a poor young girl—It costs a lot to get married. What can they do?

MANDERS. What should they do? Well, Mr. Alving, I'll tell you what they *ought* to do. They ought to stay away from each other in the first place,—that's what!

OSWALD. That talk won't go far with warm-blooded young people in love.

MRS. ALVING. That's for sure!

MANDERS. *(Ignoring this)* And this is tolerated by the authorities! They allow this to happen openly! *(Confronting* MRS. ALVING*)* Do you still think I had no reason to be concerned about your son's involvement in these circles? Outright indecency and apparent acceptance—!

OSWALD. Let me tell you something, Reverend. I have been a regular guest in several of these "illicit" homes on Sundays—

MANDERS. Even on Sunday!

OSWALD. Yes, for that day was set aside for Man to enjoy. But never in these homes have I heard an offensive word; and, furthermore, I've never seen behavior there that one could call indecent. No, but do you know where I have witnessed indecency in artistic circles?

MANDERS. No, God forbid!

OSWALD. Well, I'll tell you anyway! I have witnessed it when one or another of your model husbands and fathers came down there to look around a little on his own—and do the artists the honor of looking in at them in their shabby little cafes. The bitter truth is that these gentlemen were able to tell us about places and things that we had never dreamed of.

MANDERS. What? Are you implying that respectable gentlemen from this country would—?

OSWALD. Haven't you heard such men when they came home again, heard them carry on about the excessive immorality abroad?

MANDERS. Yes, of course—

MRS. ALVING. So have I.

OSWALD. Well, you can take their word for it. They are experts on it. *(Clasping his head)* Oh—that beautiful sense of liberty that is part of life down there—and they only cheapen it!

MRS. ALVING. You mustn't over-excite yourself, Oswald. It isn't good for you.

OSWALD. You're right, Mother. It's bad for the health to get so damned worked up about it. Well, I'll take a calming stroll before dinner. Pardon me, Pastor, I know you can't see it that way; but I simply had to speak out. *(He exits through the door Up Right.)*

MRS. ALVING. My poor boy—!

MANDERS. Yes, I agree with you there. So this is what he's come to!

MRS. ALVING. *(Looking at him in silence)*

MANDERS. *(Pacing back and forth)* He called himself the prodigal son. For shame—shame.

MRS. ALVING. *(Continuing to look at him)*

MANDERS. And what do you have to say about all this?

MRS. ALVING. I say that Oswald is right in every word that he said.

MANDERS. *(Standing still)* Right? Right? With such principles?

MRS. ALVING. All alone out here I have come to hold the same beliefs, Reverend. But I've never had the courage to admit it. Very well, now my son will speak for me.

MANDERS. You are a woman to be pitied, Mrs. Alving. I must have a serious talk with you. I will not speak to you as your business advisor or consultant, nor as you or your late husband's old friend. No, it is your minister who stands before you now as once before he stood in the hour of your greatest temptation.

MRS. ALVING. And what does the pastor have to say to me?

MANDERS. First let me refresh your memory. This is the appropriate time. Tomorrow is the tenth anniversary of your husband's death; tomorrow his memorial will be unveiled; tomorrow I shall address the whole assemblage; but today I wish to speak to you alone.

MRS. ALVING. Very well, Reverend, go ahead.

MANDERS. Need I remind you how after less than a year of marriage you found yourself on the very edge of catastrophe? That you deserted your house and home—and fled from your husband—yes, Mrs. Alving, ran, ran away and refused to return to him even though he begged and pleaded with you?

MRS. ALVING. Have you forgotten how grievously unhappy I was during that first year?

MANDERS. That is the true stamp of a rebellious spirit! To expect happiness here on earth. What right have we mortals to expect happiness? No, we must do our duty, Mrs. Alving! And your duty was to cleave fast to your husband whom you had chosen and to whom you were bound in bonds of holy matrimony.

MRS. ALVING. You know very well the sort of life Alving led at that time; the utter depravity he indulged in.

MANDERS. I know very well what was said of him; and I
would be the last to approve of his youthful misconduct,
if the rumors were true. But it is not a wife's place to judge
her husband. It was instead your duty to bear humbly the
cross which a higher power had seen fit to burden you
with. But instead you cast down that cross in rebellion,
deserted the poor stumbling one you should have sup-
ported, at the risk of your own good name and reputation,
and—and very nearly ruined other reputations as well.

MRS. ALVING. Others? *One* other, you mean.

MANDERS. It was extremely inconsiderate of you to seek
refuge with me.

MRS. ALVING. With our minister? With our friend?

MANDERS. Especially for that reason.—Yes, you can
thank God that I had the necessary firmness,—that I succeeded in talking you out of your hysterical intention and
that it was granted me to lead you back to the path of duty,
and home to your lawful husband.

MRS. ALVING. Yes, Pastor Manders, that most certainly
was your doing.

MANDERS. I was merely a tool in the hand of a higher
power. And has it not proven a blessing to you throughout
your life that I was able to guide you to this pathway of
duty and obedience? Was it not as I said it would be? Didn't
Alving turn aside from his erring ways like the proper man
he was? Did he not share with you a loving and blameless
life for the remainder of his days? Didn't he become a
public benefactor and didn't he lift you up until you became his partner in everything he undertook? And a most
capable partner, too.—Oh, I am aware, Mrs. Alving, that
you deserve *that* credit.—But now I come to the second
great mistake in your life.

MRS. ALVING. What do you mean by that?

MANDERS. Whereas once you shirked your duty as a
wife, now you have shirked your duty as a mother.

MRS. ALVING. Oh—!

MANDERS. All your life you have been ruled by an unfortunate spirit of self-indulgence. You've always yearned

for a life free of laws and restraints. Anything which has been unpleasant in your life you have thrown off without conscience or consideration, as if it were a burden you had the right to unload. You didn't like being a housewife and so you deserted your husband. You found it tiresome being a mother, and so you turned your child over to strangers.

MRS. ALVING. Yes, it's true. I did, that.

MANDERS. And for that reason you also became a stranger to him.

MRS. ALVING. No, no, I am *not*!

MANDERS. That you *are*; it must be. Just why is he back again? Think it over, Mrs. Alving. You had greatly sinned against your husband;—you admit that by raising this memorial to him down there. Can't you also admit that you have sinned against your son? There may still be time to lead him back from the ways of temptation. Turn back yourself and save what still can be saved in him. For thou art *(Raising his forefinger)* I say unto thee, Mrs. Alving, thou art a guilty mother!—I have found it my duty to tell you this.

(There is a silence.)

MRS. ALVING. *(Slowly and with control)* Now you have had your say, Reverend; and tomorrow you will speak publicly at my husband's memorial service. I'm not going to speak tomorrow. But I will have a few words with you now, as you have had with me.

MANDERS. Of course, you wish to make excuses for your behavior—

MRS. ALVING. No, I will merely tell you what took place.

MANDERS. Oh—?

MRS. ALVING. Everything that you have just told me about me and my husband and our life together after you, as you put it, led me back to the path of duty—you know absolutely none of that from your own observation. From that moment you—who had been a daily visitor in our house—did not set foot in it again.

MANDERS. You and your husband moved from town immediately afterwards.

MRS. ALVING. Yes, and you never came out here while my husband was alive. It was business that finally forced you to visit me, when you undertook to manage the orphanage affairs.

MANDERS. *(Quietly and uncertainly)* Helena—If this is a reproach, I must ask you to consider—

MRS. ALVING. —your responsibility, your duty to your position, yes. And also I was a "wayward" wife. One must always be careful how one deals with reckless females.

MANDERS. Dearest—Mrs. Alving, this is a terrible exaggeration—

MRS. ALVING. Yes, let's let that be. What I wanted to say was that you had no personal basis on which to judge my behavior as a wife.

MANDERS. Very well; but what of that?

MRS. ALVING. Well now, Henrik, now I will let you know the truth. I have sworn to myself that one day I would let you know. You alone!

MANDERS. And what is this truth?

MRS. ALVING. The truth is that my husband died just as depraved as he had lived all his days.

MANDERS. *(Fumbling for a chair)* What are you saying?

MRS. ALVING. After nineteen years of marriage he was as depraved—at least in his desires—as he was before you married us.

MANDERS. Those youthful escapades—those irregularities—excesses if you like, you call that a depraved life!

MRS. ALVING. That's the expression our doctor used.

MANDERS. I don't understand.

MRS. ALVING. It doesn't matter.

MANDERS. It makes my head swim. Your entire marriage—all those years you lived with your husband were nothing but a false front!

MRS. ALVING. Nothing but that. Now you know.

MANDERS. This—I can't accept it. I can't believe it! Can't grasp it! But how is it possible that—? How on earth could it be kept secret?

MRS. ALVING. That was an endless struggle for me day after day. After Oswald was born I thought things were better with Alving. But not for long. And then I had to fight a double battle, fight for the very life of me to see that no one should know the kind of man my son had for a father. And you know how charming Alving could be. No one could believe anything but good of him. He was one of those people whose behavior couldn't tarnish his reputation. But then, Henrik—I want you to know this, too—then came the most disgusting thing of all.

MANDERS. More disgusting than that?

MRS. ALVING. I had put up with him even though I knew how he was carrying on away from the house. But when he brought disgrace right within these walls—

MANDERS. What? Here?

MRS. ALVING. Yes, here in our very home. In there *(Points to the first door on the right)*—in our dining room was where I first found out. I was doing something in there and the door was not closed. I heard the maid come up from the garden with water for the plants there.

MANDERS. Yes—?

MRS. ALVING. Shortly after that I heard Alving come in also. He whispered something to her. And then I heard— *(With a short laugh)* Oh, the thought of it still makes me want to laugh and cry too—I heard my own maid whisper: "Let me go, sir! Leave me be!"

MANDERS. What a cheap prank on his part! But that's all it was, a prank, Mrs. Alving. Believe me on that.

MRS. ALVING. It didn't take long for me to find out what to believe. He got what he was after—and the girl soon couldn't hide the consequences, Pastor Manders.

MANDERS. *(In shock)* All that in this house! In this house!

MRS. ALVING. I have endured much in this house. To keep him home evenings—and at night, I had to keep him company during long drunken spells up in his room, I had to sit there alone with him, clinking glasses and drinking with him and listening to the filthy things he said. I actually had to fight with him to get him into his bed—

MANDERS. *(Shaken)* How could you endure it all?

MRS. ALVING. I had to for the sake of my little boy. But when that final insult came; when my very own maid—;

then I swore to myself: This must stop! And then I took charge in this house—completely—over him and over everything else. For now I had a weapon against him, you see; he didn't dare complain. That is when I sent Oswald away. He was nearly seven years old and beginning to notice things and ask questions like children do. I couldn't bear that, Henrik. I was sure the child would be poisoned by merely breathing the air in this unclean home. That's the reason I sent him away. And now you know why he was not allowed to come back home while his father was alive. No one can ever know what that cost me.

MANDERS. Yours has been a trying life.

MRS. ALVING. I could never have held out if it had not been for the work here. Yes, I can say I have worked! All the additions to the estate, all the improvements, all the new ways of doing things for which my husband received such wide and favorable publicity,—Do you think he had the energy for any of them? *He,* who lay all day on a sofa reading last year's honors lists! No, I'll tell you this, too, it was *I* who drove him on when he would chance to have one of his lucid moments, and *I* was also the one who had the whole load when he began his dissipations again and collapsed into helpless self-pity.

MANDERS. And to this man you are raising a memorial.

MRS. ALVING. There you see the power of a guilty conscience.

MANDERS. Guilty—? What do you mean?

MRS. ALVING. I was certain that the truth would eventually come out and be believed. The object of the orphanage was to dispel any rumors and cover all doubt.

MANDERS. You most certainly have succeeded there, Mrs. Alving.

MRS. ALVING. I also had *another* motive. I had made my mind up that Oswald, my own son, should not inherit anything at all from his father.

MANDERS. You mean it's Alving's fortune that—?

MRS. ALVING. Yes. The total amount that I have put into the orphanage year by year adds up to—I have been figuring it very carefully—the amount which once made Lieutenant Alving in younger days such a good catch.

MANDERS. I understand—

MRS. ALVING. It was my purchase price—I won't have any of that money fall into Oswald's hands. My son shall inherit all he has from me. *not just $— values*

(OSWALD *enters Up Right. He has left his hat and coat in the hallway.*)

MRS. ALVING. (*Going to him*) Back already? My dear, dear boy!

OSWALD. Yes. I couldn't get far in this never-ending drizzle. But I hear dinner is ready. That's great!

REGINA. (*Enters from dining room with a package*) This package was delivered for you, madam. (*Hands it to her*)

MRS. ALVING. (*Glancing at* PASTOR MANDERS) Music for tomorrow's ceremony I suppose.

MANDERS. Hmm—

REGINA. And dinner is served.

MRS. ALVING. Good; we'll be in presently. I only want to—(*She begins to open the package.*)

REGINA. (*To* OSWALD) Would Master Alving prefer red or white wine?

OSWALD. Both, Miss Engstrand.

REGINA. *Bien—*; very good, sir. (*She exits into the dining room.*)

OSWALD. I'd better help her uncork those bottles—(*He follows her into the dining room. The door remains half open after him.*)

MRS. ALVING. (*Having opened the package*) I was right; here are copies of the songs, Pastor Manders.

MANDERS. (*With folded hands*) How will I ever deliver the address tomorrow with a free conscience now that I—!

MRS. ALVING. Oh, you'll find a way.

MANDERS. (*Quietly so as not to be heard in the dining room*) Yes, there must be no scandal. *of life married sacrificed*

MRS. ALVING. No. And *now* this long painful comedy can come to an end. From the day after tomorrow it will be as if the dead man never lived in this house. There will be no one here but my boy and his mother.

(From the dining room comes the crash of a falling chair.)

REGINA's *voice. (In a harsh whisper)* Oswald! Are you mad! Let me go!

MRS. ALVING. *(Starting violently in terror)* Oh—!

(She stares wildly at the half-open door. Off stage we hear OSWALD *clearing his throat; he begins to hum. Then we hear a bottle being uncorked.)*

MANDERS. *(Excitedly)* What is going on in there. What is it, Mrs. Alving?

MRS. ALVING. *(Hoarsely)* Ghosts. The couple from the sun room—they've returned.

MANDERS. What are you saying! Regina—? Is *she*—?

MRS. ALVING. Yes. Come. Not a word—!

(She grips PASTOR MANDERS's *arm and walks unsteadily toward the dining room.)*

Act Two

(The same room. A drizzling mist still covers the land-scape in the background. Pastor Manders *and* Mrs. Alving *enter from the dining room.)*

Mrs. Alving. *(Still in the doorway)* I'm glad you enjoyed it, Pastor. *(Speaking back into the dining room)* Aren't you coming also, Oswald?

Oswald. *(From within)* No thanks; I thought I'd go out for a walk.

Mrs. Alving. Yes, do that; it seems to have let up for a bit. *(Closing the dining-room door she goes to the hall door and calls.)* Regina!

Regina. *(Off stage)* Yes, ma'am?

Mrs. Alving. Go down to the work room and help with the decorations.

Regina. Very well, ma'am.

Mrs. Alving. *(Assures herself that Regina has gone; then closes the door)*

Manders. Can he hear anything in there?

Mrs. Alving. Not a thing while the door is closed. Besides he's going out.

Manders. I'm still in a state of shock. I don't know how I managed to eat a bite of that marvelous dinner.

Mrs. Alving. *(Controlling her uneasiness, paces up and down)* I don't either. But what are we going to do?

Manders. Yes, what is to be done? I really don't know; I have no experience with this sort of thing.

Mrs. Alving. I am convinced that no harm has come of it yet. *Regina's not pregnant yet*

Manders. No, Heaven forbid. But the situation is a thoroughly indecent one.

Mrs. Alving. It's no more than a passing fancy on Oswald's part. You can be sure of that.

She excuses son as pastor excused her husband.

MANDERS. Yes, well, as I said I really don't know about such things but I really do think—

MRS. ALVING. She must get out of the house. At once. That's for sure—

MANDERS. Yes, I understand.

MRS. ALVING. But where to? It wouldn't be proper to—

MANDERS. Where to? Home to her father, of course.

MRS. ALVING. To whom?

MANDERS. To her— No, but Engstrand isn't her—But, Good Lord, woman, how could that be possible? Surely you are mistaken?

MRS. ALVING. Unfortunately, I know I am not. Johanna came and confessed to me—and Alving was in no position to deny it. So there was nothing to be done but hush the matter up.

MANDERS. Yes, that was wise.

MRS. ALVING. The girl left my service immediately and was given a very generous sum to remain quiet. She took care of everything else herself after she got to town. First she looked up her old acquaintance Engstrand and let it be known, I'm sure, how much money she had. Then she made up a story for him about a foreigner who supposedly had anchored his yacht here that summer. The result was that she and Engstrand had a hasty marriage. Well, you know, you performed it yourself.

MANDERS. But I can explain, I assure you. I remember very well the time when Engstrand came to make the arrangements. He was so perfectly contrite and accused himself bitterly for the guilt of that sinful little indulgence with his sweetheart.

MRS. ALVING. Well, he had to take the blame on himself.

MANDERS. But it was dishonest! And I was the victim! I would never have believed it of Jacob Engstrand. No, I will certainly reprimand him for this; *that* he had best be prepared for.—And the immorality of such a marriage! For the sake of money—! How much did the girl have?

MRS. ALVING. Three hundred dollars.

MANDERS. Think of that—for a mere three hundred dollars to go and marry oneself to a fallen woman!

MRS. ALVING. What can you say about me, who let myself be married to a fallen man!

MANDERS. But, God help us;—What kind of expression is that? A fallen man!

MRS. ALVING. Do you believe Alving was purer when I went to the altar with him than Johanna was when Engstrand married her?

MANDERS. But that is an entirely different situation—.

MRS. ALVING. Not so different. Oh, yes, there was quite a difference in the price:—a mere three hundred dollars against an entire fortune.

MANDERS. But how can you even compare the two? After all, you were following the call of your heart and the advice of your family.

MRS. ALVING. *(Not looking at him)* I thought you were aware of the direction my heart was calling me at that time.

MANDERS. *(Aloof)* Had I been aware I would not have been a daily guest in your husband's house.

MRS. ALVING. Well, all the same, I did not take my own advice on the matter.

MANDERS. Then you did the proper thing: you took the advice of your nearest relations: your mother and your two aunts.

MRS. ALVING. Yes, that much is true. The three of them worked the whole thing out for me. Oh, it's incredible how they calculated it so that it appeared to be utter stupidity to turn down such an offer. If Mother could only see what those dreams of glory have come to.

MANDERS. The outcome cannot be blamed on anyone. And you may be certain of this, that your marriage was in full accordance with orderly legal practice.

MRS. ALVING. *(By the window)* Yes of course, law and order! I often think *that* is the very thing that causes all the unhappiness in this world.

MANDERS. Mrs. Alving, how sinful of you!

MRS. ALVING. Yes, that may be; but I can no longer be bound by all these petty considerations. I cannot! I must work my way free of them.

MANDERS. What do you mean?

MRS. ALVING. *(Drumming her fingers on the windowsill)*
I should never have covered up the life Alving led. But I
didn't dare do anything else at the time—I kept thinking
of others. That's what a coward I was.

MANDERS. Coward?

MRS. ALVING. If anyone had found out they would have
said: "Poor fellow, it's no wonder he carries on so; after
all, his wife ran out on him!"

MANDERS. Perhaps they would have some justification
there.

MRS. ALVING. *(Staring steadily at him)* If I had the
strength of character I would like to have, I would call in
Oswald and say: "Listen, my son, your father was a de-
generate—"

MANDERS. But, bless me—.

MRS. ALVING. —and then tell him everything I have told
you—word for word.

MANDERS. You shock me, Mrs. Alving!

MRS. ALVING. Yes, I know; I see that! These thoughts
even shock me. *(Moving away from the window)* That's the
coward in me.

MANDERS. You call it cowardly to do what was your simple duty and obligation? Have you forgotten that a child
should love and honor his father and mother.

MRS. ALVING. Let's not talk in generalities. Let us say
rather: Should Oswald love and honor Chamberlain Alving?

MANDERS. Surely there is a voice in the heart of a mother
that tells her not to destroy her son's ideals?

MRS. ALVING. But what about the truth?

MANDERS. Yes, but what about ideals?

MRS. ALVING. Oh—ideals, ideals! If only I weren't such
a coward!

MANDERS. Don't cast out ideals, woman, lest the curse
fall back on your own head. Now take Oswald's case. Oswald does not believe in many ideals, I fear. But this much
I have observed: his father stands to him as an ideal being.

MRS. ALVING. You're right about that.

MANDERS. And this very image of him was created and nurtured in him by you yourself through your letters.

MRS. ALVING. Yes, I felt it was an obligation, my duty; and for that reason I lied to my son year after year. Oh, what a coward, what a coward I've been!

MANDERS. You have planted a pleasant illusion in your son, Mrs. Alving—and your conscience should treasure the result.

MRS. ALVING. Hmm. That one can never know.—But I won't allow him to amuse himself where Regina is concerned. He will not be allowed to make that poor girl unhappy!

MANDERS. No, Good God, that would be terrible!

MRS. ALVING. If only I knew whether he were truly serious, and if it would make him happy.

MANDERS. Serious?

MRS. ALVING. But that can't be; Regina is just not the type.

MANDERS. What do you mean?

MRS. ALVING. If I weren't such a miserable coward I would simply say to him: Marry her, or do what you will; just don't be dishonest about it.

MANDERS. Merciful Heavens—! A legal marriage! How terrible—! I never heard—!

MRS. ALVING. Never heard, you say? Put your hand on your heart, Pastor Manders, and swear that you are not aware that here in this parish are other couples as closely related as these two?

MANDERS. I simply do not understand you.

MRS. ALVING. Oh yes you do.

MANDERS. Well, you're thinking of chance occurrences where—. Yes, unfortunately, everyday family life is not always as pure as it could be. But in such cases one can't be positively certain,—Here, on the contrary—; you, the mother would actually allow your own—

MRS. ALVING. But I don't *want* to. I would give anything in the world to prevent it; that's what I am trying to say.

MANDERS. Because you are a coward as you put it. But if you were not such a coward—! God in heaven,—such a shocking arrangement!

MRS. ALVING. Yes, we all come from such an arrangement originally, they tell us. And who was it that arranged things like that in this world, Pastor?

MANDERS. I do not intend to discuss such questions with you, woman; you are far from being in the correct spiritual frame of mind. You dare to say that it is cowardly of you—!

MRS. ALVING. Let me explain. I have a dreadful fear that deep down inside me is something ghostlike which I can never exorcise.

MANDERS. What did you call it?

MRS. ALVING. "Ghost-like." When I heard Regina and Oswald in there it was like ghosts haunting me. I almost think we are all ghosts, Pastor Manders. It is not only what we have inherited physically from our fathers and mothers that walks in us; it's all sorts of old dead ideas and all kinds of old lifeless beliefs. They are not alive in us; but they remain there just the same . . . and we cannot purge ourselves of them. I have only to take a newspaper and read it and I see ghosts behind the words. The whole country must be full of them. They are as thick as grains of sand. And we are all miserably afraid to expose them to the light.

MANDERS. Aha,—This is the harvest of your reading. Fine fruit indeed! Oh these loathsome, rebellious, free-thinking writers!

MRS. ALVING. You are wrong, dear Pastor. You yourself are the one who first set me thinking; and for that I thank and bless you.

MANDERS. Me!

MRS. ALVING. Yes, when you forced me to do what you called my "duty and obligation," when you praised as right and proper that which my whole self rebelled against as an abomination. Right then I began to examine the seams in your reasoning. I only wanted to pick at a single knot; but when I had worked the *one* loose, the whole fabric unravelled. And then I saw that it was machine made.

MANDERS. *(Quietly, shaken)* Can this be the reward of the hardest struggle of my life?

MRS. ALVING. You should call it your most pitiful defeat.

MANDERS. It was the supreme victory of my life, Helena; victory over myself.

MRS. ALVING. It was a crime against us both.

MANDERS. When you came to me in your confusion and cried: "Here I am! Take me!" Then I besought you: "Woman, go home to your lawful husband!" Was that a crime?

MRS. ALVING. I believe it was.

MANDERS. We don't understand each other.

MRS. ALVING. No, not any longer.

MANDERS. Never—Not even in my most secret thoughts, have I thought of you except as another man's wife.

MRS. ALVING. Oh—Is that so?

MANDERS. Helena—!

MRS. ALVING. It's so easy to forget the self one used to be.

MANDERS. Not I. I am the same self I always was.

MRS. ALVING. *(Changing the subject)* Yes, yes. Well— Let's talk no more of the good old days. You are sitting here up to your ears in commissions and committees; and I am at war with ghosts from within and without.

MANDERS. I'll be glad to help rid you of the outward ones at least. After everything I have heard from you today my conscience won't allow me to let a young unprotected girl remain in your house.

MRS. ALVING. Wouldn't it be best to see that she was provided for? I mean—a decent marriage?

MANDERS. Undoubtedly. I believe that would be just the thing for her. Regina is just now at the age where—; well, I don't really know about these things but—.

MRS. ALVING. Regina matured early.

MANDERS. Yes, didn't she? I seem to recall that she was noticeably well filled-out from a physical viewpoint when I prepared her for confirmation. For the present, however, she must return home; with her father to look out for her—.

No, but Engstrand is not—, That he—that *he* would hide the truth from me like that!

(There is a knock at the hall door.)

MRS. ALVING. Who could *that* be? Come in!

ENGSTRAND. *(Wearing his Sunday suit, in the doorway)* I beg your pardon, ma'am, but—

MANDERS. Aha! Hmm—

MRS. ALVING. Oh, is it you, Engstrand?

ENGSTRAND. —None of the maids are around so I took the liberty myself to knock.

MRS. ALVING. Yes, yes, come in. You wish to talk to me?

ENGSTRAND. *(Coming in)* No, thank you, ma'am. It's really the pastor I wish to have a word with.

MANDERS. *(Walking up and down)* Hmm, indeed. You wish to talk to me? Do you really?

ENGSTRAND. Yes, I'd be so terribly grateful if—.

MANDERS. *(Stops in front of him)* Well, out with it. What is it you want?

ENGSTRAND. Yes, it's just this, Reverend, sir: that now we've all been paid up down there. Many thanks, ma'am. —And now everything is all set; and so I thought it would only be right and proper if we who have worked together so well all this time—I thought we should finish off with some devotions this evening.

MANDERS. Devotions? Down at the Orphanage?

ENGSTRAND. Yes, unless the pastor doesn't think it appropriate—.

MANDERS. Oh, yes indeed I do, but—hmm—

ENGSTRAND. I myself have been in the habit of holding little prayer sessions down there of an evening.

MANDERS. Have you?

ENGSTRAND. Yes, now and then; sort of edifying you might say. But then I am a poor, humble layman and haven't the real gift. God help me,—and so I said to myself, seeing as how Pastor Manders is out here, well—.

MANDERS. Now, look here, Mr. Engstrand, first I have a few questions to ask you. Are you in the right frame of mind for such an undertaking? Is your conscience free and clear?

ENGSTRAND. Oh, God help us, I would rather not talk about conscience, Reverend.

MANDERS. But that is just what we are going to talk about. What do you say to that?

ENGSTRAND. Well, conscience—that can be very painful sometimes.

MANDERS. So at least you admit that. But will you also admit to me—the truth about Regina?

MRS. ALVING. *(Quickly)* Pastor Manders!

MANDERS. *(Reassuringly)* Leave this to me—.

ENGSTRAND. Regina! Jesus, now you're trying to scare me! *(Looking at* MRS. ALVING*)* There isn't nothing happened to Regina is there?

MANDERS. Let's hope not. But what I meant was, what's the truth about you and Regina? You call yourself her father, don't you? Well?

ENGSTRAND. *(Uncertainly)* Yes—hmm—Your Reverence already knows all that about me and poor Johanna.

MANDERS. You can't bend the facts around any longer. Your dead wife confessed the whole thing to Mrs. Alving before she left her service.

ENGSTRAND. Well I'll be God da—! She really did, did she?

MANDERS. You are found out, Engstrand.

ENGSTRAND. And she gave her word and swore on the Bible—.

MANDERS. On the Bible!

ENGSTRAND. Well, she gave her word, and so very piously.

MANDERS. And all these years you've hidden the truth from me. Hidden it from *me*, who trusted you in everything.

ENGSTRAND. Yes, I'm afraid I did.

MANDERS. Have I deserved this from you, Engstrand? Have I not always stood ready to advise and assist you—in any way that I was able? On your honor, now! Is that not so?

ENGSTRAND. Many a time I would have had tough going if it hadn't been for the pastor.

MANDERS. And this is how you repay that debt. Getting me to enter a false statement in the church registry and holding back from me for years the information which you owed both to me and to the cause of truth. Your behavior has been completely without defense, Engstrand; and from now on we are through.

ENGSTRAND. *(With a sigh)* Yes, well, very well, I understand.

MANDERS. Yes, but don't you even intend to justify yourself?

ENGSTRAND. How was I to know she'd get herself in worse trouble by talking about it? Just suppose, Pastor, Sir, if you was in the same difficulty as poor Johanna—.

MANDERS. I?

ENGSTRAND. Jesus, I didn't mean exactly like that. But what I meant is suppose the pastor had something it was better to hide from the prying eyes of his fellow man we might say. We men mustn't judge a poor woman too harshly, Your Reverence.

MANDERS. But that is just the point. It's *you* that I am reproaching.

ENGSTRAND. Then, sir, may I put to you a small question?

MANDERS. Yes, yes, what is it?

ENGSTRAND. Is it not right and fitting that Man should strive to lift up the fallen?

MANDERS. Yes, that's obvious.

ENGSTRAND. And is it not also a man's duty to stand by his word?

MANDERS. Most certainly it is; but—.

ENGSTRAND. That time when Johanna was unlucky enough to get in trouble because of this Englishman—or maybe he was an American or a Russki as they call 'em— well, she came right in to town, poor wretched thing, she had turned me down a couple of times before; she wouldn't even look at anyone unless they was real handsome, she wouldn't; and I had this here defect in my leg. Sure, Pastor, you remember how I had ventured up into a dance hall where those sailors was carrying on and having what you might call a drunken orgy. And when I tried to admonish them to come and be born again—.

MRS. ALVING. *(By the window)* Hmm—.

MANDERS. I know, Engstrand, the unredeemed creatures threw you down the stairs. You've told me about it before. You bear your injury with honor.

ENGSTRAND. I haven't let it make me arrogant, sir. But as I was about to say, she came right to me to pour out her troubles, with all her tears and sobbing away. You can believe, sir, it went right to your heart to hear her.

MANDERS. To the *heart,* Engstrand? Well, and so?

ENGSTRAND. Well, so I told her: "This American is a carefree wanderer adrift on life's great ocean. He is. And you, Johanna," I says, "You have sinned a great sin and have been cast down into the gutter. But Jacob Engstrand," says I, "he stands upright on both honest legs, he does."—Well, that was sort of a parable you see, Your Reverence.

MANDERS. I understand you very well. Go on.

ENGSTRAND. Well, so right then I lifted her up and made an honest women of her so that no one could know the errant ways she had been led into by that foreigner!

MANDERS. All of that was very fine of you to do. But I can not approve of the fact that you allowed yourself to accept money for it—.

ENGSTRAND. Money? I? Not a cent!

MANDERS. *(Looking questioningly towards* MRS. ALVING*)* But—!

ENGSTRAND. Oh, yes—just a moment; now I remember. Johanna did have a little cash after all. But I wouldn't have nothing to do with *that.* "Shame!" I says, "Mammon, this is the wages of sin, this is; this filthy gold—or cash; whatever it was—we'll toss it right back in the American's face," I said. But he was already gone and disappeared across the wide seas, Your Reverence.

MANDERS. Was he now, my good man?

ENGSTRAND. Yes, indeed. And so we agreed, I and Johanna, that the money should go to bring up the child, and *that's* what we did; and I can give a good accounting for every cash dollar of it.

MANDERS. Well this puts things in an entirely different light.

ENGSTRAND. That's the whole story, Your Reverence. And I'm not afraid to say I've been a right good father to Regina, as far as I've been able to—for I am but a fragile man, I'm sorry to say.

[margin note: manders modest]

ENGSTRAND. Now, now, my dear Engstrand—

ENGSTRAND. But I'll tell you this; I've brought up the child and lived tenderly with poor Johanna and ran my household according to the Good Book. But it wouldn't ever come into my head to go to Pastor Manders and blow my own horn about how I had gone and done such a thing, not me. No, when such happens to Jacob Engstrand he keeps it to himself. I'm sorry to say, that's not the way with some, you know. But when I go to Pastor Manders I always have enough guilt and weakness of my own to tell him. For I said it just now and I say it again: A man's conscience can be an ugly thing at times.

MANDERS. Give me your hand, Jacob Engstrand.

ENGSTRAND. Oh, Lord, Reverend, Sir—.

MANDERS. Always self-effacing. *(Forcibly squeezing his hand)* There, now.

ENGSTRAND. And now if I was to beg the pastor's forgiveness in order to—.

MANDERS. You? No, on the contrary; it is I who should be begging you for forgiveness—.

ENGSTRAND. Oh, Lord no.

MANDERS. Yes, indeed, and I do it with all my heart. Forgive me that I ever misjudged you so. And if there were only some way I could show you the sincerity with which I regret this and of the genuine goodwill I feel for you—.

ENGSTRAND. Do you really want to do that?

MANDERS. It would give me the greatest pleasure—.

ENGSTRAND. Well, there's a really good opportunity just now. With the blessed money I've managed to put aside out here I've been thinking of founding a sort of home for sailors in town.

MRS. ALVING. You have?

ENGSTRAND. Yes, like this here, some sort of an asylum you might say. Manifold are the temptations for the sailor who wanders ashore. But in this house with me there it would be like having a father to look out for them, I thought.

MANDERS. What do you say to that, Mrs. Alving.

ENGSTRAND. I don't have very much to start with, God only knows; but if someone could stretch out a charitable hand, well—.

MANDERS. Yes, yes, let us examine that more closely. Your undertaking interests me deeply. But go along now and get things ready down there, and light some candles to brighten the place up. We will share some inspiring moments, my dear Engstrand; for now I am certain you are in the right frame of mind for it!

ENGSTRAND. I think I am, yes. And so, goodbye, Mrs. Alving, and thanks for everything; and take real good care of Regina for me. (*Wiping a tear from his eye*) Poor Johanna's child—hmm, it's a funny thing about that—but it's just like she's grown up to be my own flesh and blood. It really does seem so. (*He bows and goes out through the hall door.*)

MANDERS. Well, what do you have to say about the man now, Mrs. Alving! *That* was quite a different explanation we were given wasn't it?

MRS. ALVING. Yes, it certainly was.

MANDERS. There, you see how extremely careful one must be not to condemn a fellow man. But it is indeed a great joy to discover that one has been mistaken. What do *you* say?

hypocrite

MRS. ALVING. I say that you are and always will be a great big child, Henrik.

MANDERS. I?

MRS. ALVING. (*Putting her hands on his shoulders*) And I feel I'd like to give you a great big hug.

MANDERS. (*Quickly freeing himself*) No, no, Lord preserve you from such fancies.—

MRS. ALVING. (*With a smile*) Oh, you needn't be afraid of me.

MANDERS. *(By the table)* Sometimes you have such exaggerated ways of expressing yourself. Just let me get these documents together and put them in my briefcase. *(He does so.)* There, now. Goodbye for now. Keep your eyes on Oswald when he returns. I'll be back to see you later. *(He takes his hat and goes out through the hall door.)*

MRS. ALVING. *(Sighs deeply, watches momentarily out the window, straightens up a few things in the room and then turns to go into the dining room, but she stops in the doorway with a soft exclamation.)* Oswald, are you still sitting at the table?

OSWALD. *(In the dining room)* I'm just finishing my cigar.

MRS. ALVING. I thought you'd gone out for a little walk.

OSWALD. In this weather?

(There is the clink of glass. MRS. ALVING leaves the door open and seats herself with her sewing on the sofa by the window.)

OSWALD. *(Still off stage)* Wasn't that Pastor Manders who just left?

MRS. ALVING. Yes, he's gone down to the orphan-asylum.

OSWALD. Hm. *(The glass and the decanter clink again.)*

MRS. ALVING. *(With a worried glance)* Oswald, dear, remember that liqueur you're drinking is very strong.

OSWALD. It helps keep out the damp.

MRS. ALVING. Wouldn't you rather come in here with me?

OSWALD. I'm not allowed to smoke in there.

MRS. ALVING. If you really want that cigar you may smoke.

OSWALD. All right I'll come then. Just a little drop more.—There, now. *(He enters with the cigar and closes the door after him. There is a moment of silence.)*

OSWALD. Where did the pastor go?

MRS. ALVING. I just told you he's down at the asylum.

OSWALD. Oh, yes, so you did.

MRS. ALVING. You should not sit so long at the table, Oswald.

OSWALD. *(With the cigar behind his back)* It's just that it's such a pleasure, Mother. *(Stroking her hair and patting her cheeks)* Think of how I feel—to come home, to sit at my mother's own table, in my mother's dining room and to taste my mother's delicious meal.

Mrs. Alving. My dear, dear boy!

Oswald. *(Somewhat impatiently walking and smoking)* And what else can I find to do here? I find it impossible to work—.

Mrs. Alving. Why is that?

Oswald. In this weather? Without even a flicker of sunlight all day long? *That's* the worst thing about it all: not being able to work—!

Mrs. Alving. Perhaps it was not such a good idea for you to come home.

Oswald. Yes, Mother. I had to.

Mrs. Alving. I'd sacrifice my happiness at having you here ten times over rather than that you should—

Oswald. *(Stopping by the table)* Tell me, Mother,—Does it really give you so much pleasure to have me home?

Mrs. Alving. I feel very fortunate!

Oswald. *(Crumpling a newspaper)* I don't think it matters to you whether I exist or not.

Mrs. Alving. How can you have the heart to say that to your own mother, Oswald?

Oswald. You have managed to get along without me so well before this.

Mrs. Alving. Yes, I have managed to get along;—that's true.

(Silence. Dusk is slowly deepening. Oswald *paces back and forth. He has put down his cigar.)*

Oswald. *(Stopping beside* Mrs. Alving*)* Mother, may I please sit on the sofa with you?

Mrs. Alving. *(Making room for him)* Yes, come here, my dear boy.

Oswald. *(Sitting)* There's something I must tell you, Mother.

Mrs. Alving. *(Anxiously)* Yes?

Oswald. *(Staring vacantly ahead)* I can't bear keeping it to myself any longer.

MRS. ALVING. Keeping what? What is it?

OSWALD. *(As before)* I couldn't bring myself to write you about it; and since coming home—

MRS. ALVING. *(Grasping his arm)* Oswald, what *is* it!

OSWALD. Yesterday and again today I tried to drive the thoughts away—to lose them, but it's no use.

MRS. ALVING. *(Standing up)* You must tell me right out, Oswald!

OSWALD. *(Draws her back down onto the sofa)* Then sit, and I'll tell you about it.—I've been complaining about being tired after the journey—

MRS. ALVING. Yes, of course! What of it?

OSWALD. But that isn't what's wrong with me; this is no ordinary fatigue.—

MRS. ALVING. *(Trying to jump up)* You aren't sick, Oswald?

OSWALD. *(Draws her down again)* Sit still, Mother. Try to stay calm. I'm not really ill; not what people ordinarily call being sick. *(Clasps his hands to his head)* Mother, my mind is going—breaking down—I will never be able to paint again!

(He throws himself into her lap with his hands over his face and bursts into uncontrollable sobs.)

MRS. ALVING. *(Pale and trembling)* Oswald! Look at me! No, no, that cannot be true.

OSWALD. *(Looks up at her in desperation)* Never again to be able to work! Never—never! Like a living death! Mother, can you imagine anything more dreadful than that?

MRS. ALVING. Unhappy boy! How could this terrible thing be happening to you?

OSWALD. *(Sitting upright again)* That's just what I haven't been able to grasp. I never led a loose sort of life. You mustn't think that of me, Mother! I never did that.

MRS. ALVING. Of course I couldn't think that, Oswald.

OSWALD. And yet it's happening to me all the same. This terrible destructive force!

MRS. ALVING. Oh, it will be all right, my dear, dear boy. You're just feeling the strain of overwork. You can take my word for it.

OSWALD. *(With great sadness)* I thought that also at first; but it's not so.

MRS. ALVING. Then tell me the whole story.

OSWALD. I want to.

MRS. ALVING. When did the first symptoms appear?

OSWALD. It was just after I had been home the last time and had returned to Paris again. I began to feel the most violent pains in my head—mostly in the back of the head, it seemed. It was as though a tight iron ring was being screwed down there around my neck and just above it.

iron collar

MRS. ALVING. *(Remembering)* Like that?

OSWALD. My first thought was that it was those same headaches that plagued me in my teens.

MRS. ALVING. Yes, yes—

OSWALD. But it wasn't that; I soon found out. I couldn't work anymore. I wanted to begin a great new painting, but it seemed as if all my powers had failed me. All my energy seemed to be paralyzed; I couldn't even seem to visualize things clearly; images swam before me—leaped around. Oh, I was in a terrible state! Then finally I went to a doctor—and from him I learned the truth.

MRS. ALVING. What do you mean?

OSWALD. He was one of the leading doctors there. I had to tell him all my symptoms; and then he began to ask me a lot of questions which seemed to me to have nothing to do with it. I couldn't figure what he was driving at—

MRS. ALVING. Well.

OSWALD. Finally he said: "It seems you have been born with a maggot inside you:"—"Wormeaten" is how he referred to me: "*Vermoulu*" in French.

MRS. ALVING. *(Tensely)* What did he mean by that?

OSWALD. I didn't understand either, and asked him to make himself clear. And then the old cynic said—*(Clenches his fists)* Oh—

MRS. ALVING. What did he say?

biblical verse

OSWALD. He said. "The sins of the father shall be visited upon the children."

MRS. ALVING. *(Slowly standing up)* The sins of the father—!

OSWALD. I almost hit him in the face—

MRS. ALVING. *(Pacing across the room)* The sins of the father—

OSWALD. *(With a melancholy smile)* Yes, what do you think of that? Naturally, I informed him that there was no chance of that. But do you think he believed *that?* No, he insisted; and it wasn't until I got out your letters and translated to him all the parts about Father.—

MRS. ALVING. What *then?*

OSWALD. Well, then of course he had to admit he was on the wrong track; and so I learned the truth. The unbelievable truth! That jubilantly happy young life my friends and I indulged in was something I should have avoided. It had completely destroyed my strength. The guilt was mine after all!

believed he'd created his own sin

MRS. ALVING. Oswald! Oh, no, don't think that!

OSWALD. There was no other possible explanation, he said. That's what is so terrible. Incurably ruined for life—for the sake of my own carelessness. All that I wanted to accomplish in the world—not even to dare think of it. Oh, if only I could live my life over—undo everything I have done! *(He throws himself face down on the sofa.)*

MRS. ALVING. *(Wringing her hands as she paces up and down struggling silently with herself)*

OSWALD. *(After a moment he looks up; raising himself on his elbow.)* If only it *had* been something I inherited—something I didn't need to blame myself for. But this! To have tossed away in such a shameful, unthinkingly reckless way your own health, happiness, everything you have in the world—your future, your life—!

MRS. ALVING. No, no my dear, blessed boy; that is not possible! *(Leaning over him)* You are not in as desperate a state as you think.

OSWALD. Oh, you don't know—*(Jumping up)* And then, Mother, that I should cause you so much sorrow! I've often hoped and prayed that you didn't really care about me as strongly as you do.

MRS. ALVING. I, Oswald? My only child! The only thing I have on earth; the only thing I could care about.

OSWALD. *(Grasps both her hands and kisses them)* Yes, yes I know. When I am here at home I know it. And that's what's so difficult about it—. But now you know. And now we won't talk about it anymore today. I can't bear to think about it for very long. *(Walking across the room)* Get me something to drink, Mother!

MRS. ALVING. Drink? What do you want to drink now?

OSWALD. Oh, whatever you have. Isn't there something chilled like brandy in the house?

MRS. ALVING. Yes, but my dear Oswald—!

OSWALD. Now, Mother, not so strict. Spoil me a little. I've *got* to have something to wash away those nagging thoughts. *(Walks up into the sun porch)* It's so—so dark and gloomy here! ~~from dishonesty~~

MRS. ALVING. *(Pulls bell cord at right)*

OSWALD. And this eternal drizzle. Week after week it goes on; a whole month and not a glimpse of the sun. All the times I've been home I don't ever remember seeing the sunshine.

MRS. ALVING. Oswald—you're thinking of leaving me!

OSWALD. Hm—*(Draws a deep sigh)* I'm not thinking about anything. I *can't* think about anything! *(Softly)* I've stopped thinking entirely.

REGINA. *(From the dining room)* You rang, ma'am?

MRS. ALVING. Yes, let's have a lamp in here.

REGINA. Right away, ma'am. It's already lit. *(Goes out)*

MRS. ALVING. *(Goes over to Oswald)* Oswald, don't keep anything back from me.

OSWALD. I'm not, Mother. *(Comes to the table)* It seems to me I've already told you plenty.

REGINA. *(Brings in a lamp and sets it on the table)*

MRS. ALVING. Now, Regina, you may go and get one of the small bottles of champagne.

REGINA. Very good, madam. *(Going out again)*

OSWALD.   *(Taking* MRS. ALVING'S *head in his hands)* That's the way it should be. I knew my Mamma wouldn't let her little boy go thirsty.

MRS. ALVING.   My poor, dear Oswald, how could I deny you anything now?

OSWALD.   *(Eagerly)* Is *that* true, Mother? Do you mean that?

MRS. ALVING.   What? Mean what?

OSWALD.   That you will not deny me any single thing?

MRS. ALVING.   But Oswald, dear—

OSWALD.   Shhhh!

REGINA.   *(Brings in a tray with a small bottle of champagne and two glasses which she sets on the table.)* Shall I open it—?

OSWALD.   No, thanks. I'll do it myself. *(*REGINA *goes out again.)*

MRS. ALVING.   *(Sitting down by the table)* What was it you meant—that I shouldn't deny you anything?

OSWALD.   *(Busy opening the bottle)* First a glass or two. *(The cork flies out; he fills one glass and prepares to pour the other.)*

MRS. ALVING.   *(Puts her hand over the glass)* Thanks— none for me.

OSWALD.   Well, for me then! *(He drains the glass, fills it again and drinks that down. Then he sits down at the table.)*

MRS. ALVING.   *(Expectantly)* Well now?

OSWALD.   *(Without looking at her)* Well, tell me—I thought you and the Pastor were so odd—hmm, so very silent at the dinner table.

MRS. ALVING.   Did you notice that?

OSWALD.   Yes, hm—*(After a short silence)* Tell me,—what do you think of Regina?

MRS. ALVING.   What do I think?

OSWALD.   Yes, isn't she splendid?

MRS. ALVING.   Oswald dear, you don't know her like I—

OSWALD.   Oh?

MRS. ALVING.   Regina, unfortunately, spent too much time at home. I should have brought her out to live with me much sooner.

OSWALD. Yes, but isn't she splendid to look at all the same, Mother? *(He refills his glass.)*

MRS. ALVING. Regina has a great many faults—.

OSWALD. Oh, yes; who cares about that? *(He drinks again.)*

MRS. ALVING. But I'm fond of her all the same; and I feel responsible for her. I wouldn't for the world have anything happen to her.

OSWALD. *(Jumping up)* Mother, Regina is the only thing that can save me.

MRS. ALVING. *(Standing)* What do you mean by that?

OSWALD. I can't bear all these painful thoughts alone any longer.

MRS. ALVING. Don't you have your mother to share the burden?

OSWALD. Yes, I thought that; and that's why I came home to be with you. But it isn't going to work, I see that; it won't. I just can't live out here!

MRS. ALVING. Oswald!

OSWALD. I must live differently, Mother. That's why I have to leave you. I don't want you to have to see that.

MRS. ALVING. My poor, sick boy! Oh, but Oswald, while you're sick like this—

OSWALD. If it were only the sickness I'd stay with you, Mother. You are my best friend in the whole world!

MRS. ALVING. You may be sure of that, Oswald!

OSWALD. *(Pacing restlessly around)* It's the sickening, nagging remorse—and then the great deathly fear. Oh— this terrible fear!

MRS. ALVING. *(Follows him)* Fear? What sort of fear? What do you mean?

OSWALD. Oh, don't ask me any more questions. I don't know. I can't even describe it to you.

MRS. ALVING. *(She goes to the right and pulls the bell cord.)*

OSWALD. What do you want?

MRS. ALVING. I want my boy to be happy, that's what I want. I don't want him to go around here brooding. *(To*

REGINA *who appears in the doorway)* More champagne. A large bottle. *(REGINA exits.)*

OSWALD. Mother!

MRS. ALVING. Don't you think we know how to live out here in the country also?

OSWALD. Isn't she splendid to watch? Such a fine body! And so healthy and full of life.

MRS. ALVING. *(Sitting down at the table)* Sit here, Oswald, so we can talk this over calmly.

OSWALD. *(Sitting down)* You don't know this, Mother, but I have done Regina a wrong that I feel I must make up for.

MRS. ALVING. You!

OSWALD. A thoughtless little thing—you might say. Really very innocent. The last time I was home—

MRS. ALVING. Yes?

OSWALD. —She was always asking me about Paris, and I would tell her this and that about life there. And then I remember one time I happened to say: "Wouldn't you like to come down there sometime yourself?"

MRS. ALVING. Yes?

OSWALD. Well, she blushed beet-red, and then she said: "Yes I really would like that." "Well, well," I replied, "Perhaps that can be arranged," or some such thing.

MRS. ALVING. And then?

OSWALD. Naturally I forgot the whole thing; but the day before yesterday when I happened to ask her if she was glad I was going to stay here so long—

MRS. ALVING. Yes?

OSWALD. She looked at me in the strangest way and asked me: "Then what has become of my trip to Paris?"

MRS. ALVING. Her trip!

OSWALD. And so I got it out of her that she had taken it all seriously, that she had gone around here thinking of me the whole time, and that she had gone to the trouble of learning French—

MRS. ALVING. That, too—

OSWALD. Mother—when I looked at this beautiful, healthy girl standing there—well, I'd never really noticed her before—But then, when she stood there looking so open and willing.—

MRS. ALVING. Oswald!

OSWALD. —It came to me that she could be the thing that would save me; for all the joy of life is in her.

MRS. ALVING. *(Startled)* The joy of life—? Can *that* save you?

REGINA. *(Enters from the dining room with a full bottle of champagne)* I'm sorry I took so long; I had to go down to the cellar—. *(She sets the bottle on the table.)*

OSWALD. And bring in another glass.

REGINA. *(Looks at him in surprise)* There's madam's glass, Mr. Alving.

OSWALD. Yes, but get one for yourself, Regina.

REGINA. *(Startled, she throws a quick glance at Mrs. Alving.)*

OSWALD. Well?

MRS. ALVING. Fetch the glass, Regina.

*(*REGINA *exits into the dining room.)*

OSWALD. *(Staring after her)* Did you watch the way she walks? So free and vigorous.

MRS. ALVING. This cannot come about, Oswald!

OSWALD. It already has. Surely you see that. It's no use to talk further.

REGINA. *(Enters with an empty glass, which she holds in her hand)*

OSWALD. You may sit, Regina.

REGINA. *(Glances questioningly at* MRS. ALVING*)*

MRS. ALVING. Sit down.

REGINA. *(Sits on a chair by the door to the dining room and holds the empty glass in her hand)*

MRS. ALVING. Oswald—What was it you were saying about the joy of life?

OSWALD. Yes, Mother, the joy of life—I don't see much of it here at home. I don't ever feel it here.

MRS. ALVING. Even when you are with me?

OSWALD. Never when I'm home. But you wouldn't understand.

MRS. ALVING. Yes, yes—I think I do—now.

OSWALD. That—and the love of one's work. Yes they're practically the same thing. But then you wouldn't be able to comprehend that either.

MRS. ALVING. Perhaps you are right, Oswald. But I'll try to listen if you explain.

OSWALD. Well, it's like this, you see: in this country people are brought up to believe that work is a curse and punishment for their sins, and that life is a misery we are best to rid ourselves of as soon as possible.

MRS. ALVING. "A vale of tears"—yes. And we certainly go out of our way to make it so.

OSWALD. But in the world out there people aren't even aware of that. No one there teaches that sort of thing any longer. They feel it is a wonderful glorious thing to be alive in this world. Mother, haven't you noticed that all of my paintings have dealt with celebrating the joy of life? Always and forever the fun of being alive? Full of light and sunshine and the air of holidays—and men with beaming, delighted expressions on their faces. It's for that reason I'm afraid to be at home here with you.

MRS. ALVING. Afraid? What have you to be afraid of here with me?

OSWALD. I'm afraid that anything I set out to do here will turn to ugliness.

MRS. ALVING. *(Looks hard at him)* Do you believe *that* is inevitable?

OSWALD. I'm certain it is. Even if I tried to live the same here at home as I did out there, it could never be the same kind of life.

MRS. ALVING. *(Who has been listening intently, raises herself up, her eyes wide and thoughtful)* I begin to see the connection now.

OSWALD. You see what?

MRS. ALVING. I see it now for the first time. And now I'm free to speak.

OSWALD. *(Standing)* Mother, I don't understand.

REGINA. *(Who also has risen)* Perhaps I should go?

MRS. ALVING. No, stay, I'm free to talk now. Now, my son, I'll tell you the whole story. And then you can make your choice. Oswald! Regina!

OSWALD. Be quiet. The pastor—

MANDERS. *(Enters by the hall doorway)* Well now, we've had a most pleasant and profitable time down there.

OSWALD. So have we.

MANDERS. We must assist Engstrand with his home for sailors! Regina will go into town with him and help with the work—.

REGINA. No thank you, Pastor, Sir.

MANDERS. *(Taking first notice of her)* What—? Here,— and with a glass in your hand!

REGINA. *(Quickly sets down the glass)* Pardon—! *(French accent)*

OSWALD. Regina is going away with me, sir.

MANDERS. Going away! With you!

OSWALD. Yes, as my wife.—If she desires it.

MANDERS. But, God help you—!

REGINA. This is not my doing, sir.

OSWALD. Or she will stay with me here if I stay.

REGINA. *(Involuntarily)* Here!

MANDERS. I am shocked by this, Mrs. Alving.

MRS. ALVING. Neither of these things will happen. For now I am free to let it all come out.

MANDERS. But you mustn't do that! No, no, no.

MRS. ALVING. Yes, I must; and I will. And no one's ideals will suffer.

OSWALD. Mother, is there something you have been hiding from me?

REGINA. *(Listening)* Listen, madam! There are people shouting out there. *(She goes up into the sun porch and looks out.)*

OSWALD. *(At the window, left)* What is the matter? Where is that light coming from?

REGINA. *(Cries)* There's a fire in the orphanage!

MRS. ALVING. *(At the window)* Burning!

MANDERS. Fire? Impossible? I was just down there.

OSWALD. Where's my hat? Oh, never mind—Father's asylum—! *(He runs out by the garden door.)*

MRS. ALVING. My shawl, Regina! It's all in flames.

MANDERS. Tremble, Mrs. Alving! Those flames are a judgment brought down on this household!

MRS. ALVING. Yes, yes, of course. Come, Regina. *(She and REGINA hurry out through the hallway.)*

MANDERS. *(Striking his hands together)* And it isn't insured! *(Exits the same way)*

Act Three

(The same room. All the doors are standing open. The lamp still burns on the table. It is dark outside with only a faint reflection of the fire to the left in the background. MRS. ALVING with a large shawl over her head stands upstage in the sun porch and looks out. REGINA, also with a shawl, stands a little behind her.)

MRS. ALVING. Completely burned. Down to the ground.

REGINA. It's still burning in the cellar.

MRS. ALVING. Why doesn't Oswald come up? There's nothing left to save.

REGINA. Should I go down there and take him his hat?

MRS. ALVING. Didn't he even take his hat along?

REGINA. *(Pointing to the hall)* No. It's hanging there.

MRS. ALVING. Well let it hang. He must be on his way up now. I'll go look for him myself. *(She goes out through the garden door.)*

MANDERS. *(Entering from the front hall)* Isn't Mrs. Alving here?

REGINA. She just went down into the garden.

MANDERS. This is the most dreadful night I have ever experienced.

REGINA. Yes, sir, isn't it a terrible tragedy?

MANDERS. Oh, don't talk about it! I don't even want to think about it.

REGINA. But how could it have happened—?

MANDERS. Don't ask me, Miss Engstrand. How would *I* know that? Are *you* also trying to—? Isn't it enough that your father—?

REGINA. What about him?

MANDERS. Oh, he's nearly driven me crazy.

ENGSTRAND. *(Enters from the hall)* Pastor Manders, Sir—!

MANDERS. *(Turning away in fright)* Are you after me here as well!

ENGSTRAND. God help me, yes—! Oh, Jesus, but this really looks bad, Your Reverence.

MANDERS. *(Walking up and down)* Indeed, indeed!

REGINA. Now what is it?

ENGSTRAND. Oh, well you see, it all began because of this here prayer service. *(Under his breath)* We've got him this time, girl! *(Aloud)* And so you see I am to blame for this awful thing Pastor Manders did!

MANDERS. But I assure you, Engstrand—?

ENGSTRAND. But there wasn't nobody but the pastor in charge of the candles down there.

MANDERS. *(Stops)* Yes, so you say. But I can't recall ever having a candle in my hand.

ENGSTRAND. But I saw as plain as anything Your Reverence take a candle and snuff it with your fingers, and throw the wick right down in the wood shavings.

MANDERS. You saw that?

ENGSTRAND. Yah, I saw that, I did.

MANDERS. That's what's so hard for me to understand. It has never been a habit of mine to put out candles with my fingers.

ENGSTRAND. Yah, it sure did look careless, it did. But it can't really be so big a loss can it, Your Reverence?

MANDERS. *(Pacing uneasily back and forth)* Oh, don't ask me!

ENGSTRAND. *(Pacing with him)* And I understand the pastor didn't have it insured?

MANDERS. *(Still walking)* No, no, no; you heard me say that.

ENGSTRAND. *(Following him)* Not insured. And then to go right down there and light a fire to the whole thing. Je-e-esus, what bad luck!

MANDERS. *(Wiping the sweat from his brow)* Yes, you may well say that, Engstrand.

ENGSTRAND. And that such a thing should go and happen to a charity institute which was going to be a service both to the town and the whole countryside, so to speak. The newspapers won't go easy with you on that one, Pastor, I don't think.

MANDERS. No, that's just what I've been thinking. That's almost the worst part of this whole thing. All these hateful attacks and accusations—? Oh, it's frightful to think of it!

MRS. ALVING. *(Coming in from the garden)* He doesn't seem to want to come away from that pit full of smoldering ashes.

MANDERS. Oh, there you are, Mrs. Alving.

MRS. ALVING. So you got out of giving your speech, Pastor Manders.

MANDERS. Oh, I would far rather—

MRS. ALVING. *(Softly)* It's just as well. That asylum would have done no good.

MANDERS. You believe that?

MRS. ALVING. Don't you?

MANDERS. But it has been a great misfortune. All the same.

MRS. ALVING. You will look on it simply as a matter of business—. Are you waiting for the pastor, Engstrand?

ENGSTRAND. *(In the hall doorway)* Yes, I guess so.

MRS. ALVING. Then sit down.

ENGSTRAND. Thanks; I'm all right standing.

MRS. ALVING. *(To* PASTOR MANDERS*)* I suppose you plan to leave now on the morning boat?

MANDERS. Yes, it leaves in an hour.

MRS. ALVING. Well please take all of these papers back with you. I don't want to hear another word about it. I have other things to think about now—.

MANDERS. Mrs. Alving—

MRS. ALVING. Later I'll send you the full power-of-attorney to settle things as you see fit.

MANDERS. I will be only too happy to take that on. However, it will be necessary to change the purpose of the trust fund, unfortunately.

MRS. ALVING. I understand, of course.

MANDERS. Yes, and so I think I'll arrange for the Solvik acreage to be provisionally turned over to the parish. The property is certainly not without some value, you see. It can always be put to some use or other. And the interest from the capital in the savings bank I can use to support some project or other that can be said to benefit the town.

MRS. ALVING. Do what you like. It makes no difference to me now.

ENGSTRAND. Remember my sailor's home, Reverend.

MANDERS. Yes, that's an idea. We'll certainly consider it.

ENGSTRAND. Consider, Hell—Oh, geez!

MANDERS. *(With a sigh)* And of course I don't know how long I will be in charge of these affairs. Not if public opinion should force me to resign. That will all depend on the results of the public hearing over the fire.

MRS. ALVING. What's that?

MANDERS. And one can't possibly predict what the results of that will be.

ENGSTRAND. *(Coming closer)* Oh, yes, one can do that. For here stands Jacob Engstrand, that's me.

MANDERS. Yes, yes, but—?

ENGSTRAND. *(More quietly)* And Jacob Engstrand ain't the man to abandon a blessed benefactor in his hour of need, as the saying goes.

MANDERS. But, my good man,—how—?

ENGSTRAND. Jacob Engstrand is like an angel sent to the rescue he is, sir!

MANDERS. No, no I couldn't accept that.

ENGSTRAND. Oh, that's how it'll be anyway. I know of one who took the blame for someone else before now, I do.

MANDERS. Jacob! *(Wringing his hand)* You are a rare individual. Well, you shall receive assistance for your seaman's home; be assured of that.

ENGSTRAND. *(Wants to talk, but is too emotional for words)*

MANDERS. *(Picking up his satchel)* Well, let's set out. We two shall travel together.

ENGSTRAND. *(At the dining-room door says quietly to RE-GINA)* Come with me, wench! You'll be as cozy as a gull in the egg.

REGINA. *(Tossing her head) Merci!* *(French accent)* *(She goes out into the hall and brings* MANDERS *his overcoat.)*

MANDERS. Farewell, Mrs. Alving! I hope that soon you will set things in this household in order and impose once more the rule of all things right and decent.

MRS. ALVING. Goodbye, Henrik!

(She goes upstage towards the sun porch as she sees OSWALD *coming in through the garden door.)*

ENGSTRAND. *(While he and* REGINA *are helping* PASTOR MANDERS *on with his coat)* Goodbye, my child. And if you should ever get in trouble, you know where Jacob Engstrand will be found. *(Softly)* Little Harbor Street, hmmm—! *(To* MRS. ALVING *and* OSWALD*)* And the house for wayfaring sailors is going to be called "Chamberlain Alving's Home." How's that? And if I can run it the way *I* have in mind it will really be a fitting memorial to the Captain, by God. *house of prostitution?*

MANDERS. *(In the doorway)* Hmm—hmm! Come along, Engstrand. Goodbye, goodbye! *(He and* ENGSTRAND *go out together through the front hallway.)*

OSWALD. *(Coming in to the table)* What house was he talking about?

MRS. ALVING. Some sort of hostelry or asylum he and Pastor Manders intend to open.

OSWALD. It'll burn down just like this one.

MRS. ALVING. What makes you say that?

OSWALD. Everything is destroyed by fire. Nothing must remain to remind people of Father. Here am I also—burning, burning down.

REGINA. *(Looks at him, startled)*

MRS. ALVING. Oswald! You shouldn't have stayed down there so long, poor boy.

OSWALD. *(Sits at the table)* Perhaps you're right.

MRS. ALVING. Let me dry your face, Oswald. You are wringing wet. *(She wipes his face with her handkerchief.)*

OSWALD. *(Standing indifferently in front of her)* Thanks, Mother.

MRS. ALVING. Aren't you tired, Oswald? Wouldn't you like to sleep?

OSWALD. *(Frightened)* No, no—not sleep! I never sleep; I only pretend to. *(In deep melancholy)* That will come soon enough.

MRS. ALVING. *(Looks worriedly at him)* Yes, my dear boy, now I am certain that you're sick after all.

REGINA. *(Breathless)* Mr. Alving is sick?

OSWALD. *(Impatiently)* And close all the doors! Oh, this deathly fear—

MRS. ALVING. Close them, Regina.

*(*REGINA *closes the doors but remains by the one to the front hall.* MRS. ALVING *takes off her shawl;* REGINA *does the same.)*

MRS. ALVING. *(Pulls a chair close to* OSWALD'S *and sits down by him)* There, now. Now I'll sit here by you—

OSWALD. Yes, do. And Regina, stay here also. Regina must always stay near me. You're going to save me, Regina. Won't you do that?

REGINA. I don't understand—

MRS. ALVING. Save you—?

OSWALD. Yes—when the time comes.

MRS. ALVING. Oswald, you have a mother here to do the saving.

OSWALD. You? *(Smiling)* You wouldn't save me from this. *(Laughing heavily)* You! Ha-ha! *(Looking seriously at her)* Though really you are the one who should do it. *(Violently)* Why are you always so formal, Regina? Why can't you call me Oswald for once?

REGINA. *(Sits quietly and hesitantly at the other side of the table)*

MRS. ALVING. And now, my poor, tortured boy, now I will remove the burden from your mind—

OSWALD. You, Mother?

MRS. ALVING. —All this torture and self blame you spoke of—

OSWALD. You think you can do that?

MRS. ALVING. Yes, now I can, Oswald. You spoke last night of the fun and joy of life, and it was as if a new light was thrown over every part of my own life.

OSWALD. *(Shaking his head)* I don't understand.

MRS. ALVING. You should have known your father when he was a young lieutenant. *He* was bubbling over with the joys of living.

OSWALD. Yes, I know.

MRS. ALVING. It was exhilarating just to look at him. There was a strength and vitality in him that was beyond control.

OSWALD. Well—?

MRS. ALVING. So this happy child full of the joy of life— he was so like a child then—found himself at home here in a little town that had no joys to offer him, only drudgery. Found himself with no purpose in life, only an official position. No matter how he tried he couldn't find something into which he could throw himself heart and soul, only routine business. He didn't even have a friend who was capable of understanding this great joy of life, only loafers and drinking buddies—

no joy in work

OSWALD. Mother—!

MRS. ALVING. So it ended as it had to end.

OSWALD. Ended? How?

MRS. ALVING. You yourself said earlier what would happen to you if you had to stay here at home.

OSWALD. Are you telling me that Father—?

MRS. ALVING. Your poor father couldn't find an outlet for his overwhelming vitality. And I certainly didn't make his home a sunny place, either.

OSWALD. Not even you?

MRS. ALVING. I had been taught about moral duty and such, and I sat here for so long and believed in it. I looked at everything as an obligation—mine and his—. I fear I made your poor father's home unendurable, Oswald.

OSWALD. Why didn't you ever write me about this?

MRS. ALVING. Before now I never saw that it was something I could tell his son.

OSWALD. Then how did you see it?

MRS. ALVING. *(Very slowly)* I saw only that your father was broken down morally and physically long before you were born.

OSWALD. *(Softly)* Oh—! *(He stands and goes to the window.)*

MRS. ALVING. And there was another matter that haunted me day in and day out:—that Regina had had every right to be in this house—like my own boy.

OSWALD. *(Turning around quickly)* Regina—!

REGINA. *(Jumping up, asks softly)* I—?

MRS. ALVING. Yes. Now you know it, both of you.

OSWALD. Regina!

REGINA. *(To herself)* So mother was like that after all.

MRS. ALVING. Your mother was a good woman in many ways, Regina.

REGINA. Yes. But she was like that all the same. Yes, I thought so every once in a while; but—Yes, ma'am, if I have your leave I'll be going at once?

MRS. ALVING. Do you really want to, Regina?

REGINA. Yes, I sure do.

MRS. ALVING. Naturally you may do as you wish, but—

OSWALD. *(Goes toward* REGINA*)* Going away now? This is where you belong.

REGINA. *Merci*, Mr. Alving;—Yes, now I suppose I should say Oswald. But this is really not the way I intended it to be.

MRS. ALVING. Regina, I have not been very honest with you—

REGINA. No, you haven't, that's for sure! If I had known Oswald was sick like that—. And also now that there can't be anything serious between us—. No, you'd better believe I'm not going to stay out here in the country and look after sick people.

OSWALD. Not even for one who is so very close?

REGINA. I should say not! A poor girl is young only once; She has to make the best of it while she can. And I also have the joy for living in me, ma'am!

MRS. ALVING. Yes, I'm afraid, so. But don't throw yourself away, Regina.

REGINA. Oh, if I do, it's only fitting. You can put it this way if you like: If Oswald takes after his father, then I take after my mother! —May I ask if Pastor Manders knows this about me?

Mrs. Alving. The Pastor knows the whole story.

Regina. *(Begins to put on her shawl)* Well then, I'd better get down to the steamboat as fast as I can. The Pastor is such a simple man to get along with; and I'm just as sure that I have as much right to the money as that dirty carpenter has.

Mrs. Alving. You are welcome to it, Regina.

Regina. *(Looks at her spitefully)* You could have brought me up like a gentleman's child. *(Tossing her head)* What the hell—it's all the same! *(With a bitter, sidelong glance at the still unopened bottle)* I'm going to get to drink champagne with gentlemen yet, I am.

Mrs. Alving. If ever you need a home, Regina, come to me.

Regina. No, many thanks, ma'am. Pastor Manders will take care of me. And if things get real bad I know a house I can call home.

Mrs. Alving. Where's that?

Regina. It's "Chamberlain Alving's Home."

Mrs. Alving. You'll destroy yourself, Regina!

Regina. Pffft! *Adieu (She curtsies and goes out through the front hall.)*

Oswald. *(Standing by the window and looking out)* Is she gone?

Mrs. Alving. Yes.

Oswald. *(Mumbles to himself)* This is madness, all this.

Mrs. Alving. *(Goes over behind him and places her hands on his shoulders)* Oswald, my dear boy,—has all of this been a shock to you?

Oswald. *(Turns to face her)* All this about Father, you mean?

Mrs. Alving. Yes your unfortunate father. I'm so afraid it may have been too much for you to take.

Oswald. Why do you feel that way? Naturally it comes as a great surprise; but there's really not much difference when you get right down to it.

MRS. ALVING. *(Taking her hands away)* Not much difference! That your father was so completely miserable?

OSWALD. Naturally I can feel sorry for *him* just like I would for anybody, but—

MRS. ALVING. Just anybody! Your own father!

OSWALD. *(Impatiently)* Oh, father—father. I didn't even know my father. I don't even remember him except that once he made me vomit.

MRS. ALVING. What a terrible thing to say! Surely a child must love his father no matter what!

OSWALD. Even if that child has nothing to thank its father for? Has never known him? Do you really believe that old wives' tale, you, who are so enlightened in other ways?

MRS. ALVING. That's just an old wives' tale—?

OSWALD. Yes, surely you see that, Mother. It's just one of those beliefs passed on in this world in order to—

MRS. ALVING. *(Shuddering)* Ghosts!

OSWALD. *(Walking across the room)* Yes, that's not a bad name for them: ghosts.

MRS. ALVING. *(Bursting out)* Oswald,—then you don't love me either!

OSWALD. At least I know you—

MRS. ALVING. Yes, know; but is that all!

OSWALD. And I'm aware of how fond you are of me; and I have to be grateful to you for that. And for all the use you can be to me now that I am sick.

MRS. ALVING. Yes, that I can be, Oswald! Oh, I could almost bless your sickness for bringing you home to me. For now I realize: you are *not* mine. I must win you.

OSWALD. *(Impatiently)* Yes, yes, yes, that's all just talk. You have to realize how sick I am, Mother. I can't bother myself about other people now; I have enough worry just thinking of myself.

MRS. ALVING. *(Quietly)* I won't complain and I'll be patient.

OSWALD. And cheerful, too, Mother!

MRS. ALVING. Yes, my dear boy, I'll be cheerful. *(Goes over to him)* Now have I freed you from all that remorse and self blame?

OSWALD. Yes, you have that. But what about the fear?

MRS. ALVING. Fear?

OSWALD. *(Again crossing the room away from her)* Regina would have done what's required for just a kind word.

MRS. ALVING. I don't understand. What is this about the fear—and about Regina?

OSWALD. Is the night almost over, Mother?

MRS. ALVING. It's close to morning. *(She looks out through the sun porch.)* Dawn is breaking high up on the mountains. And it is clearing up, Oswald! In a little while you shall see the sun.

OSWALD. I'm looking forward to that. Oh there are still so many things for me to look forward to and live for—

MRS. ALVING. I know there are!

OSWALD. Even if I'm not able to work, well—

MRS. ALVING. Oh, you'll soon be able to work again, my dear. Now that you no longer have those nagging and oppressive thoughts to dwell on.

OSWALD. No, it's a good thing you were able to rid me of those. And now if I can only get past this one last thing— *(Sitting on the sofa)* Let's settle it now, Mother—

MRS. ALVING. Yes, let's. *(She pushes an armchair over to the sofa and sits near him.)*

OSWALD. —And meanwhile the sun will rise. And then you will see it all. And I will no longer have this fear.

MRS. ALVING. What is it I will see?

OSWALD. *(Without listening to her)* Mother, didn't you say last night that if there was anything in the world I wanted you to do for me I only had to ask?

MRS. ALVING. Yes, I certainly did!

OSWALD. And you stand by your word, Mother?

MRS. ALVING. I promise you that, my dearest, my only boy. You are the only thing I live for, you alone.

OSWALD. Yes, yes, well then listen—You are strong,—you have great control, Mother. I know that. Now you must sit there quietly while I tell this.

MRS. ALVING. But what could be so terrible that—!

OSWALD. Please don't scream, do you hear? Promise me that? We'll just sit and talk quietly about it. Will you promise me, Mother?

MRS. ALVING. Yes, yes, I promise. Only tell me!

OSWALD. All right. All of this talk about being tired— and about work—all that is not the real sickness—

MRS. ALVING. Then what is it really?

OSWALD. The sickness I have is an inheritance, it— *(points to his forehead and says very softly)* it is in here.

MRS. ALVING. *(Almost speechless)* Oswald! No—no!

OSWALD. Don't scream. I couldn't bear that. Yes, you see, it sits in here and waits. And from here it can break loose at any time, any hour.

MRS. ALVING. Oh, how horrible!

OSWALD. Keep calm now. That's just the way it is—.

MRS. ALVING. *(Leaping up)* It isn't true, Oswald! It's impossible! It can't be true!

OSWALD. I've already had *one* attack down there. It was soon over. But when I found out the condition I had been in while it lasted, this great fear came over me and began to haunt me; and that's why I came home as quickly as I could.

MRS. ALVING. So *that's* the fear—!

OSWALD. Yes, it's so unspeakably repulsive, you see. Oh, if it had only been an ordinary terminal illness—Because I'm really not afraid to die; though, of course, I'd like to live as long as I can.

MRS. ALVING. Yes, yes, Oswald, that you must!

OSWALD. But this is really so repulsive. To be turned into a baby again, who must be fed, who must be—Oh,— I can't describe it!

MRS. ALVING. A child has its mother to care for it.

OSWALD. *(Jumping up)* No, never. That is exactly what I will not have! I can't bear the thought that I might be like that for years—grow old and grey. And you might die and leave me in the meantime. *(Sits in* MRS. ALVING's *chair)* I might not die all at once the doctor said. He called it sort of a softening of the brain. *(Smiling sadly)* I think the sound of that is so lovely. It makes me think of cherry-red velvet draperies—so soft and delicate to the stroke.

Mrs. Alving. *(Shrieks)* Oswald!

Oswald. *(Springs up again and strides across the room)* And now you have taken Regina from me! If only I still had her. She was the thing that would have saved me, I know.

Mrs. Alving. *(Going to him)* What do you mean by that, my dearest? Is there anything in the world I wouldn't do to save my boy?

Oswald. When I had recovered from the last attack down there the doctor told me that when it comes again— and it will come again—there will be no further help.

Mrs. Alving. What a heartless thing to say—

Oswald. I made him tell me. I told him that I had to make certain preparations in advance—*(Smiling cunningly)* and that I have done. *(Takes a little box out of his breast pocket)* Mother, do you see this?

Mrs. Alving. What is that?

Oswald. Morphine powders.

Mrs. Alving. *(Looks at him in horror)* Oswald—my boy?

Oswald. I've managed to get together twelve capsules—

Mrs. Alving. *(Trying to grab the box)* Give it to me, Oswald!

Oswald. Not yet, Mother. *(Puts the box back in his pocket)*

Mrs. Alving. I'll never live through this.

Oswald. You'll have to. If Regina were here now I'd have told her how things are with me—and asked her to do that last service. She'd have helped me; I'm sure of that.

Mrs. Alving. Never!

Oswald. When the horror would come over me and she would see me lying there helpless as a baby, involuntary, hopeless, lost—beyond all help—

Mrs. Alving. Never in the world would Regina do it!

Oswald. Oh yes she would. Regina was so beautifully carefree. It wouldn't take her long to get tired of looking after an invalid like that.

MRS. ALVING.   Then thank God Regina is not here!

OSWALD.   Yes, well then, now you must be the one to do me this last service, Mother.

MRS. ALVING.   *(Shrieking out)* I!

OSWALD.   Who is nearer to me than you?

MRS. ALVING.   I! Your mother?

OSWALD.   For that very reason.

MRS. ALVING.   I, who gave you life?

OSWALD.   I didn't ask you for life. And what sort of a life have you given me? I don't want it. You will have to take it back!

MRS. ALVING.   Help! Help! *(She runs out into the hallway.)*

OSWALD.   *(Going after her)* Don't leave me! Where are you going?

MRS. ALVING.   *(In the hallway)* I'll get you a doctor, Oswald! Let me out!

OSWALD.   *(Also off stage)* You're not going out. And no one's coming in. *(We hear a key in the lock.)*

MRS. ALVING.   *(Coming in again)* Oswald! Oswald,—my child!

OSWALD.   *(Following her)* If you have a mother's love for me—then how can you allow me to suffer from this inexpressible fear?

MRS. ALVING.   *(After a moment's silence, says with a controlled voice)* Here is my hand on it.

OSWALD.   Then you will—?

MRS. ALVING.   If it becomes necessary. But it *never* will. No, no that will never happen!

OSWALD.   Yes, let us hope for that. And let us live together as long as we are able. Thank you, Mother. *(He settles into the armchair which MRS. ALVING has moved over by the sofa. The day is breaking, the lamp still burns on the table.)*

MRS. ALVING.   *(Cautiously approaching him)* Now are you feeling calmer?

OSWALD.   Yes.

MRS. ALVING.   *(Leaning over him)* This has just been a frightening figment of your imagination, Oswald. Only your imagination. All this excitement has been too much. But now you will get some rest. You're at home with your own mother, my dearest. Just point to anything you want and you shall have it just like when you were a little boy.— There now, now the attack is over. See how easy that was! Oh, I knew it.—And look, Oswald, what a lovely day we have in store? Sunshiney-bright! Now you'll really see your home. *(She crosses to the table and puts out the lamp. The sun rises. The glacier and snowy peaks in the background glitter in the morning light.)*

OSWALD. *(Sitting in the armchair facing away from the background; he does not move. Suddenly he says.)* Mamma, give me the sun.

MRS. ALVING. *(By the table, starts, and looks at him)* What did you say?

OSWALD. *(In a dull toneless voice)* Sun—the sun.

MRS. ALVING. *(Goes over to him)* Oswald, are you feeling all right?

OSWALD. *(Seems to shrivel up in the chair; all of his muscles relax; his face is expressionless; his eyes stare out emptily.)*

MRS. ALVING. *(Trembling with fright)* What is it? *(Screaming out)* Oswald! What's wrong? *(Throws herself on her knees before him and shakes him)* Oswald! Oswald! Look at me! Don't you know me?

OSWALD. *(Tonelessly as before)* Sun—the sun.

MRS. ALVING. *(Jumps up in despair; tears at her hair with both hands and cries)* I can't bear it! *(With a terrified whisper)* I can't bear it! Never! *(Suddenly)* Where did he hide them? *(Fumbles quickly across his breast)* Here! *(Drawing back a few steps and cries out)* No; no; no!—Yes! No; no! *(She stands a few steps away from him, with her hands twisted in her hair and stares at him in speechless horror.)*

OSWALD. *(Sits motionless as before repeating)* Sun—sun.

Miss Julia

A Naturalistic Tragedy

AUGUST STRINDBERG

1888

Translated from the Swedish by
Thaddeus L. Torp

Characters

Miss Julia, *the Count's daughter, 25 years old*
Jean, *the Count's valet, 30 years old*
Kristine, *the Count's cook, 35 years old*

(The action takes place in the kitchen of the Count's estate in rural Sweden on Midsummer Night.) *

(A large kitchen, the ceiling and walls of which are disguised with draperies and hanging wreaths. The back wall, running at an angle upstage from the left, holds shelves filled with copper, iron, and tin utensils; the shelves are swagged with decorative paper. Over to the right most of a large, arched doorway leading outside can be seen. Through its glass double doors one can see a fountain with a cupid, lilac bushes in bloom, and the tops of some poplar trees. lone spring

*Midsummer Night in Scandinavia is usually not celebrated on the year's longest day, June 21, but is transferred to the Christian feast day for St. John, June 23–24. Midsummer Night is marked with an exhausting all-night-long festival of drinking, dancing, and a general relaxation of inhibitions. Because of the belief that the night of the solstice, when the sun's path is reversed, attracts pagan spirits, freshly gathered herbs and flowers are hung in garlands on door lintels and around the necks of farm animals for protection. (Note Strindberg's description of the kitchen setting with its swagged wreaths and flowers.) Other beliefs associated with this magical evening concern the casting of spells and potions to conjure images of a young person's true love. (Jean assumes this is what Julia and Kristine are plotting, but it is only a folk recipe to abort the dog.)

The romantic fairy-tale events of this magical summer night were almost a tradition in Scandinavian plays. Ibsen used this night for the events of his short play *St. John's Night* (1852) which concerns an elf-like character who confuses two young couples with his supernatural revelations. In England, where the traditions were brought by Anglo-Saxon and Scandinavian settlers, major examples of the fables appear in dramas, such as Shakespeare's *A Midsummer Night's Dream* and Sir James Barrie's *Dear Brutus*.

In a nook to the left a large cookstove and part of its hood are visible. The hearth is garlanded with birch branches; the floor is strewn with juniper greens. To the right the end of a white-pine table, where the servants eat, and a few chairs jut onto the stage. On the table's end stands a great Japanese spice pot holding a large bouquet of lilac blossoms.

An icebox, a work table, a washstand, a large old-fashioned bell above the door used to summon the servants, and the mouthpiece of a speaking tube to the side of the door are also prominent in the room.

KRISTINE *stands by the stove frying something in a skillet; she wears a light, cotton party dress which she protects with a kitchen apron.* JEAN *enters. He wears livery and carries a pair of large riding boots with spurs which he sets before himself with a flourish on the floor.)*

JEAN. Tonight Miss Julia has gone wild again; absolutely wild!

KRISTINE. So, you're back?

JEAN. I drove the Count to the station and when I came back by the barn I went in for a dance. The young mistress was hogging the dance floor with the gamekeeper. But when she saw me she rushed right over and ordered me to waltz her ladyship. And she's still waltzing out there now—like nothing I've ever seen before. She's gone mad!

KRISTINE. She's always been like that, but it's been worse these last few weeks, since her engagement was broken off.

JEAN. Yeah, well, what's that have to do with this? He was a good man even if he wasn't rich. Ach! All those people care about is appearances. *(He seats himself at the head of the table.)* Still it's strange that the young lady—um—would rather stay at home with the servants, you know?, than go with her father to spend the holiday with her own relatives.

KRISTINE. She's probably embarrassed over the uproar about her ex-fiancé.

JEAN. Sure! Still he was quite a man. Do you know what happened, Kristine? I saw it all, but I didn't want anybody to know.

KRISTINE. No, you saw it?

JEAN. Yes, I did—They were down in the stable yard one night and the young lady was "training" him as she called it—Do you know what that was? Well, she made him jump over her riding crop just like you teach a dog. He jumped two times and got a cut of the whip each time; when the third time came he grabbed the riding crop out of her hand and broke it in a thousand pieces; then he just cleared out!

[handwritten margin note: she was treating her fiancé like an animal]

KRISTINE. So that's how it happened! No-o-o!

JEAN. Yes, that's what caused it—But what have you got there for me, Kristine?

KRISTINE. *(Dishing up the contents of the pan, she sets it before* JEAN.*)* Oh, it's a little kidney that I carved out of the veal carcass.

JEAN. *(Sniffing the food)* Marvelous! This is my prime *delice! (Feeling the plate)* You should have warmed the plate!

KRISTINE. You're pickier than the Count when you get right down to it. *(Running her hands caressingly through his hair)*

JEAN. *(Angrily)* Leave my hair alone. You know what that does to me.

[handwritten margin note: affair/flirt]

KRISTINE. Well, well, it was only a little love pat! *(*JEAN *eats.* KRISTINE *opens a bottle of beer.)*

JEAN. Beer, on Midsummer Eve; No, thanks. I've got something better for myself. *(Pulls out of the table drawer a bottle of red wine with a gold seal)* Gold seal, you see!— Get me a glass. One with a stem when you drink *pure!*

KRISTINE. *(Crosses over to the stove and sets a small pan on the fire)* God help the one who marries you! You're so finicky!

JEAN. Talk away! You'd be more than happy to land a man like me; and it hasn't caused you pain to have everyone calling me your sweetheart! *(Tasting the wine)* Good! Very good! Just a tiny bit too cool! *(Warming the glass with his hand)* We bought this in Dijon. And it cost us four francs a liter, that's without the bottle; and then there was import duty!—*Now* what are you cooking? What a smell!

KRISTINE. Oh, it's some damned brew Julia wants to feed to Diana.

JEAN. You need to refine your language, Kristine! Why stand there and cook for her mutt on a holiday evening? Is it sick?

KRISTINE. Oh yah, she's sick all right! She got loose with the gatekeeper's pug—and now she's in trouble—and you know the mistress won't allow that.

JEAN. The young lady is so stuck up in some ways and doesn't take enough pride in others, just like the Countess when she was alive, she got along best in the kitchen or the cow-barn, but she wouldn't ride behind only *one* horse; she went around with smudges on her linen cuffs but insisted on wearing cuff buttons with coronets on them.— The young lady, since we're talking about her, doesn't take proper care of herself. I might even venture to say she has no refinement. Just now when she was dancing in the barn she cut in on the gamekeeper, and Anna and took him for herself. You wouldn't see us behave like that; but that's how it is with the gentry, when they want to degrade themselves—they really get low-down! But she is magnificent to look at! Splendid! Ah! Such shoulders! And—*etcetera!*

KRISTINE. Oh, sure, she's got nothing to brag about! I've heard what Clara has to say about that; she dresses her.

JEAN. Pfffh, Clara! You women are always jealous of each other! I've been out riding with her . . . I've watched her dancing!

KRISTINE. Listen, Jean! Will you dance with me when I'm finished here?

JEAN. Sure, of course.

KRISTINE. Promise me?

JEAN. Promise? When I say I'll do it, I'll do it! And thanks for the meal. It was very good! *(He corks the bottle.)*

THE YOUNG LADY.° *(Appears in door way, talking to someone off stage)* I'll be right back! Go on without me!

JEAN. *(Hides the bottle in the drawer, and rises respectfully)*

JULIA. *(Enters and crosses to KRISTINE by the mirror)* Well! Is it ready?

KRISTINE. *(Signals that JEAN is present)*

JEAN. *(Gallantly)* Do you two have a female secret?

JULIA. *(Striking his face with her handkerchief)* That's for your nosiness.

JEAN. Ah, what a delightful smell of violets!

JULIA. *(Coquettishly)* Fresh! So he knows something about perfumes also? And dancing, he's good at that . . . Well, don't peek! Go away.

JEAN. *(Saucily, politely)* Is that some kind of troll soup for Midsummer Night you ladies cook up? Something to tell the future by, or reveal the man who's fated for you.

JULIA. *(Sharply)* To see *that,* one really must have sharp eyes! *(To KRISTINE)* Pour it in a small bottle and cork it well.—Come and dance the Schottisch with me, Jean . . .

JEAN. *(Hesitates)* I don't wish to be impolite, but I've promised the next dance to Kristine . . .

JULIA. Well, she can get another; how's that, Kristine? Won't you lend Jean to me?

KRISTINE. That's not for me to say. If the mistress is so gracious, then it's not his place to deny her. Go on, already! And be thankful for the honor!

JEAN. If I may speak frankly without meaning to offend, I wonder if it's wise of your ladyship to dance two times in succession with the same partner, those folks will start hinting . . .

JULIA. *(Flares up)* About what? What sort of hints? What do you mean?

JEAN. *(Complacently)* If the lady does not wish to understand, I will put it more plainly. It looks bad to show

°Strindberg always refers to her as *Fröken,* young lady, in the play's text. I will use her name, according to American custom. See "Notes on the Translation."

preference toward one of your servants when the others would like to be honored in the same way . . .

JULIA. Preference! What an idea! I'm astonished! I, the mistress of this house, honor the servants' dance with my presence, and when I actually wish to dance, I'm determined that it be someone who knows how to lead, and because of this they'll make fun of me?

JEAN. As the lady commands! I am at your service!

JULIA. *(Softer)* Don't regard it as a command! Tonight we ought to celebrate like happy human beings and leave social classes behind! There, offer me your arm!—Never fear, Kristine! I shall return your sweetheart to you!

JEAN. *(Offers his arm to* JULIA *and leads her out)*

*

Pantomime°

(To be acted as though the actress were alone; when required, she turns her back to the audience; never looking out into the auditorium; she must never hurry for fear the audience will get restless. KRISTINE *is alone on stage. In the distance a Schottisch tune played on a violin is faintly heard. She hums along with the tune; cleans up after* JEAN, *washes the plate at the kitchen table, wipes it and puts it in the cupboard. After that she takes off her cook's apron, takes a little mirror from a drawer, and stands it up against the flower pot on the table; lighting a candle and warming a hairpin she uses it to curl the hair on her forehead. Next she goes to the door and listens. After that she returns to the table. Discovering the handkerchief which* JULIA *has left behind she picks it up, sniffs it, smoothes it out absent-mindedly, stretches it, spreads it out, folds it, and so forth.)*

 realtime

*

JEAN. *(Entering alone)* Yes, she is crazy! The way she dances! What do you think, Kristine?

°The *"Pantomime"* and later *"Ballet"* (p. 90) are deliberate structural experimentation by Strindberg who seems to eschew curtains or blackouts to depict the passage of time in the naturalistic format.

Kristine.   Oh, well, it's her time of the month now and
she always acts peculiar. But come and dance with me now,
huh?

Jean.   You aren't mad at me for deserting you . . . ?

Kristine.   No—Not for such a little thing, you know that;
besides, I know my place . . .

Jean.   *(Puts his arm around her waist)* You're such an
understanding girl, Kristine, and you will make a good
wife . . .

Julia.   *(Entering; unpleasantly surprised at what she sees;
but she acts with forced gaiety)* Now there's a charming
cavalier—running away from his lady.

Jean.   On the contrary, Julia, I have, as you perceive,
returned to the one I deserted.

Julia.   *(Changing her tone)* You know, no one dances like
you.—But why do you wear your livery on a holiday night.
Take that off at once!

Jean.   Then I must ask your ladyship to step outside a
moment, my black coat is hanging over here . . . *(Crossing
to the right with a gesture)*

Julia.   Are you embarrassed for me? Just to change coats!
Go into your room and then come back! Or else stay here
and I'll turn my back on you.

Jean.   With your permission, your ladyship! *(Crossing to
right farther off; we should see one of his arms as he changes
coats.)*

Julia.   *(To Kristine)* Listen Kristine: are you and Jean
engaged? He seems quite free with you.

Kristine.   Engaged? Well sort of! We call it that.

Julia.   Sort of!

Kristine.   Well, Miss, you yourself had a fiancé and . . .

Julia.   Well yes, but we were really engaged . . .

Kristine.   But it didn't work out all the same . . .

Jean.   *(Enters in a black frock coat and derby)*

Julia.   *Très gentil; monsieur Jean! Très gentil!*

Jean.   *Vous voulez plaisanter, madame!*

Julia.   *Et vous voulez parler Français!* Where did you
learn that?

JEAN. In Switzerland while I was *sommelier* at one of the largest hotels in Lucerne!

JULIA. But you really look like a gentleman in that coat! *Charmant! (She sits at the table.)*

JEAN. Oh, you flatterer!

JULIA. *(Offended)* Flatter who—you?

JEAN. My natural modesty forbids my thinking that you could be speaking genuine compliments to me, and therefore I must assume that you are exaggerating or as some call it flattering!

JULIA. Where have you learned to use words like that? You must have attended the theatre a lot?

JEAN. Yes, I've managed to get around!

JULIA. But weren't you born near here?

JEAN. My father was a laborer on the county attorney's farm over there, and I can remember seeing the young lady as a child; of course you took no notice of me!

JULIA. I can't truthfully remember.

JEAN. There was one particular time . . . but I can't tell you about that!

JULIA. Oh, do it!

JEAN. No! Another time perhaps.

JULIA. Another time means not at all. Is it that naughty?

JEAN. It isn't naughty, but telling it isn't easy!— Look there! *(Points to* KRISTINE *who has fallen asleep in a chair by the stove.)*

JULIA. She'll make a docile wife, that one! But beware, she probably snores!

JEAN. No, but she talks in her sleep.

JULIA. *(Cynically)* How do you know she talks in her sleep?

JEAN. *(Impudently)* I've heard it! *(A pause during which they study one another)*

JULIA. Why don't you sit down?

JEAN. That would not be proper in your presence!

JULIA. But if I should command it?

JEAN. Then I'd obey!

JULIA. Then sit—No, wait! Can you give me something to drink first?

JEAN. I don't know what we have here in the icebox. I'm afraid there's only beer.

JULIA. Only, you say! I have such simple tastes that I prefer it to wine.

JEAN. *(Takes a bottle of beer from the icebox, and uncaps it; finds a glass and plate in the cupboard and serves it formally)* At your service!

JULIA. Thank you! Won't you have a drink yourself?

JEAN. I don't care much for beer, but if my mistress commands!

JULIA. Commands!—I should think a proper gentleman would want to keep his lady company.

JEAN. That is exactly as it should be! *(Opens another bottle, takes a glass)*

JULIA. Now a proper toast to my health!

JEAN. *(Hesitates)*

JULIA. I think the great big man is blushing!

JEAN. *(On his knee with mock solemnity; raises his glass)* To my sovereign lady's health!

JULIA. Bravo!—Now you must kiss my shoe and everything will be perfect.

JEAN. *(Hesitates, but takes a hold of her foot and gives it a light kiss)*

JULIA. Excellent! You should have been an actor.

JEAN. *(Standing)* This can't go on any longer, Julia; someone might come in and see us.

JULIA. What's the matter with that?

JEAN. People would talk, that's all! And if you knew how busy their tongues were just now . . .

JULIA. What did they say? Tell me!—Sit down now!

JEAN. *(Sitting)* I don't want to hurt you, but they used expressions—that cast reflections of a sort that . . . oh, you know! You're no longer a child, and when one sees a woman alone drinking with a man—especially if he's a servant—at night—well then.

JULIA. Then, what? Besides we are hardly alone. Kristine is right here.

JEAN. Yes, sleeping!

JULIA. Then I'll wake her. *(Standing)* Kristine! Are you asleep?

KRISTINE. *(Mumbles in her sleep)* Bla—bla—bla!

JULIA. Kristine—She is asleep all right!

KRISTINE. *(In her sleep)* The Count's boots are polished—put the coffee right on, right now, right now—huh, huh—pooh!

JULIA. *(Pinches her nose)* Wake up, won't you?

JEAN. *(Sternly)* You shouldn't disturb the sleeping.

JULIA. *(Sharply)* What?

JEAN. She's very likely tired from standing by the stove all day. Her sleep deserves respect . . .

JULIA. *(Changing tone)* Those are fine thoughts—It does you honor.—Thank you. *(Gives* JEAN *her hand)* Come out now and pick some lilacs for me. *(During the following scene* KRISTINE *wakes up. Moving as though asleep she exits right as though to go to bed.)*

JEAN. With you, Miss?

JULIA. With me!

JEAN. That wouldn't do! Absolutely not!

JULIA. I can't fathom you. What could have put such thoughts in your head?

JEAN. It's what they will think!

JULIA. What? That I am enamored of a valet?

JEAN. I'm not a conceited man, but it's been known to happen—and to the people nothing is sacred.

JULIA. You think like an aristocrat, I believe!

JEAN. Yes, and I am.

JULIA. You see it as a step down for me . . .

JEAN. Never step down, miss, listen to me now! No one will believe you willingly stepped down; people will always say that you fell down!

JULIA. I think better of these people than you do! Come and prove it—Come! *(She looks him up and down.)*

JEAN. You are a strange one!

JULIA. Perhaps, but you are also!—When you get right down to it everything is strange! Life, mankind, everything is muck that floats, floats on the water till it sinks, sinks! I have a dream that keeps recurring to me and just now I'm reminded of it. I scramble to the top of a pillar, and I'm sitting there trying to figure out how to get down, but I don't have the nerve to jump, I'm losing my hold and I long to fall off, but I don't fall. But there can be no rest for me until I do get down, no rest until I am down, down on the ground. And when I reach the ground then I want to be deep in the earth—Haven't you felt like that?

JEAN. No! In my dream I'm lying under a high tree in a dark forest. I want up, up to the top so I can see out over the sunlit landscape, bright with the sun, and rob the bird's nest up there of its golden eggs. And I climb but the trunk is too thick, too smooth, and it is so far to the first branch— But I know that if I could only get to that first branch, I could go right to the top like a ladder. So far I haven't reached it, but I will, even if only in my dreams!

JULIA. Here I sit and chatter about dreams with you! Come on! It's only out into the park! *(She offers him her arm and they start out.)*

JEAN. We must sleep on nine midsummer blossoms tonight to make our dreams come true, Miss Julia! *(They turn in the doorway.* JEAN *puts his hand up to his eye.)*

JULIA. Let me see what's in your eye!

JEAN. Oh it's nothing—only some dirt—it will soon be gone.

JULIA. My sleeve rubbed against it; sit down and let me help you! *(Takes him by the arm and sets him down; takes his head and bends it backwards; with the corner of her handkerchief tries to get the cinder out)* Sit still now, perfectly still! *(Slaps his hand)* There! Follow my orders—I think he's trembling, the great big strong man! *(She strokes his biceps with her hands.)* With arms like this!

JEAN. *(Warning)* Miss Julia!

JULIA. Yes, *Monsieur* Jean!

JEAN. *Attention! Je ne suis qu'un homme.*

JULIA. Can't you sit still!—There! Now it's gone. Kiss my hand and thank me.

JEAN. Listen, Miss Julia!—Kristine has gone to bed now!—Won't you listen to me?

JULIA. Kiss my hand first.

JEAN. Well you'll have no one to blame but yourself!

JULIA. For what?

JEAN. For what? Are you still a child at twenty-five? Don't you know it's dangerous to play with fire?

JULIA. Not for me; I'm insured!

JEAN. Not for that! And if you were you'd still have to be wary of inflammables in the vicinity. *fire was feared*

JULIA. I suppose that's you?

JEAN. Yes! Not because of who I am, but because I am young and a man—

JULIA. And attractive to look at—such unbelievable vanity! A Don Juan perchance! Or else a Joseph! Upon my soul I think he is a Joseph! — ? *Biblical reference*

JEAN. You think that?

JULIA. I almost fear it.

(JEAN walks boldly to her in order to take her by the waist and kiss her.)

JULIA. *(Cuffs his ear)* How dare you!

JEAN. Was that serious or not?

JULIA. Serious.

JEAN. Then that other was also serious. Your playing around is getting too serious and that spells danger! Now I'm tired of play and I ask to be excused to finish my work. The Count must have his boots on time and it's after midnight already.

JULIA. Put away the boots!

JEAN. No! It's the work I'm paid to do. I'm not under contract to be your playmate, and I won't ever become that, I have too high a regard of myself for that.

JULIA. You are a proud one!

JEAN. In some ways; in others not at all.

JULIA. Have you ever been in love?

JEAN. We don't use that expression. I've been attracted to a lot of girls, and one time I even got sick because I couldn't get the one I wanted: sick you know like some prince in *The Arabian Nights* who can't even eat or drink at all because of yearning!

JULIA. Who was it?

(JEAN is silent.)

JULIA. Who was it?

JEAN. You'll never make me tell.

JULIA. If I were to ask as an equal, as a—friend! Who was it?

JEAN. It was you.

JULIA. *(Sitting down)* This is priceless . . . !

JEAN. Yes, you said it! It was priceless!—that was the story I wasn't able to tell a minute ago. But now I will! Do you know how the world looks from underneath?—No, you don't. Like hawks and falcons, men never see their backs because they are always soaring so high up there. I lived in a laborer's shack with seven brothers and sisters and a pig out there on the drab plain where there isn't a single tree! But from our windows we could see that wall around the grounds of the Count's estate here and, over the top, apple trees. That was the Garden of Eden, and there stood many a fierce angel with flaming swords guarding it. But all the same I and some other boys found our way to the Tree of Life—now do you despise me?

JULIA. Oh! Stealing apples, that's something all boys do.

JEAN. You may say that, but you despise me all the same! Nonetheless, another time I got into this Garden of Eden with my mother in order to weed the onion beds. Near the vegetable garden stood a Turkish pavilion, shaded by jasmine and overgrown with honeysuckle, I didn't know what it was used for, but I had never seen such a beautiful building. People went in and came out again, and one day the door stood wide open. I sneaked up and saw the walls covered with pictures of kings and emperors, and there were red curtains at the windows with fringe on them— now you know the place I'm talking about.° I— *(Breaks off a lilac and holds it under* MISS JULIA's *nose)* I had never

°The outhouse for the estate is evidently elaborately decorated to disguise its lowly use. The interdependence of manure and flowers is a constant symbol in Strindberg's writings.

been in the estate mansion house and had seen nothing but the church—but this was more beautiful; no matter where my thoughts wandered they always came back there. And so gradually I developed a desire to experience completely the pleasure of—*enfin*, I sneaked in, gazed and admired. Then someone came to use it. There is only one exit for you fine folk; but I had to find another, and I had no choice but to get out underneath.

(JULIA *has picked up the lilac, she lets it fall on the table.*)

JEAN. Then I ran, right through a thornhedge of raspberry bushes, raced across the strawberry beds, and came out in the rose garden. That's where I caught sight of a pink dress and a pair of white stockings—It was you! I got down under a pile of weeds, right down under, imagine, among thistles and nettles and wet and smelly compost. And I looked up and saw you walking among the roses, and I got this idea: If it is possible for a thief to get to heaven and dwell among angels, then it is strange that a laborer's child here on God's earth cannot get into the park and play with the Count's daughter.

JULIA. *(Sadly)* Do you think all poor children have the same thoughts you did?

JEAN. *(Hesitates at first, then speaks with conviction)* If they *are* poor—yes—naturally! Naturally!

JULIA. It must be a terrible misfortune to be poor.

JEAN. *(With deep hurt and strong emphasis)* Oh, Miss Julia! Oh!—A dog is allowed to lie on the Countess's sofa, a horse can have his nose stroked by the young lady's hand, but a servant—*(Changing tone)* oh well, it's possible to find one made of different stuff who pulls himself up in the world; but how often does that happen? However, do you know what I did then? I jumped in the millstream with all my clothes on, was pulled out and given a spanking. But the following Sunday when Father and everyone else in the house went to Grandma's I fixed it so I could stay home. And then I scrubbed myself with soap and hot water and put on my best clothes and went to church so I could see you. I saw you and went home determined to die; But I wanted to die beautifully and pleasantly, without pain, I remembered that it was dangerous to sleep under an elderberry bush. We had a big one, and it was in full bloom. I robbed it of all the blossoms and made myself a bed in the oat bin. Have you ever noticed how smooth oat grains are? Soft to the touch as human skin . . . ! Well, I shut myself in and closed my eyes; and was very sick when I woke up. But I did not die, as you can see. What I wanted—I didn't know! There was no hope of winning you—but you were a symbol of the hopelessness of trying to rise above the class into which I was born!

JULIA. You tell that story beautifully, you know! Did you go to school?

JEAN. A little. But I've read a lot of novels and I go to the theatre. Beside that I've listened to the talk of the upper classes and from them I've learned the most.

JULIA. Of course!

JEAN. I've heard plenty when driving the carriage or rowing the boat. Once I listened in on you, Miss Julia, and one of your girlfriends—

JULIA. Ah!—What did you hear?

JEAN. Well, it's not easy to repeat. But I was more than a little surprised, and I couldn't figure out where you learned those words. Perhaps at bottom there isn't as much difference as men think between the classes.

JULIA. For shame! We don't sleep together like you when we are engaged.

JEAN. *(Giving her a fixed look)* Oh come now Miss Julia—Don't play the innocent to me—.

JULIA. He was worthless, the one I gave my love to.

JEAN. You always say that—afterwards.

JULIA. Always?

JEAN. Always! I think I've heard the same words several times before on just such occasions.

JULIA. When was that?

JEAN. The one I just spoke of! And then before that . . .

JULIA. *(Stands)* Hush! I won't hear any more!

JEAN. Your girlfriend wouldn't either I remember! I beg your permission to go to bed.

JULIA. *(Softly)* Go to bed on Midsummer Night!

JEAN. Yes! Dancing with that crowd out there is no attraction to me.

JULIA. Take the key to the boat and row me out on the lake. I want to see the sun come up.

JEAN. Is that wise?

JULIA. It sounds as though you are worrying about your reputation.

JEAN. And why not? I don't like being made fun of, and I wouldn't want to be discharged without references, because I'm trying to better myself. And then, I feel I have some obligation to Kristine.

JULIA. Ah, yes, now it's Kristine . . .

JEAN. Yes, but also you. —Take my advice, go up and go to bed!

JULIA. Shall I take orders from you?

JEAN. Just this once, for your own sake! I beg you! It's late. Sleepiness makes a person act drunk and hot headed! Get to bed! Besides—if I hear correctly—that crowd out there is coming here looking for me. If they find us here then you're lost!

(CHORUS is heard off stage singing a risqué song as they approach.)

> Two country girls came out for the air.
> Ring-ding-a-ding, Ding-a-ding.
> One was all wet, but we won't say where!
> Ring-ding-a-down-Hey-down.
>
> They bragged and flaunted their father's money.
> Ring-ding-a-ding, Ding-a-ding.
> Dollars had they, but no sense—that's funny.
> Ring-ding-a-down-Hey-down.
>
> "We bring you our virgin wreaths!" they said.
> Ring-ding-a-ding, Ding-a-ding.

But one had misplaced her maidenhead.
Ring-ding-a-down-Hey-down.

(margin handwritten note: contradicts Jes)

JULIA. I know the common folk and I love them, and they all love me. Let them come and you'll see!

JEAN. No, Miss Julia, they don't love you. They take your food and then spit behind your back! Believe me. Listen to them—can't you hear what they're singing!—No, you don't hear them!

JULIA. *(Listening)* What are they singing?

JEAN. Obscene verses. And it's you and me they have in mind!

JULIA. Disgraceful! Shame! How treacherous—

JEAN. A crowd is always cowardly. In such a battle the best advice is to run.

JULIA. Run? But where? We can't go out there. And we can't go into Kristine's room.

JEAN. Well, into mine then. Necessity knows no law. You can trust me; I am your genuine, sincere, and respectful friend.

JULIA. But what if they look in there?

JEAN. I'll lock the door, and if anyone tries to break in, I'll shoot!—Come! *(On his knees)* Come!

JULIA. *(With deep meaning)* You promise me . . . ?

JEAN. I swear!

(JULIA exits hastily to the right. JEAN, with a sudden flash of ardor, in hot pursuit)

*

Ballet

(Led by a fiddler the country folk enter. They wear their best and most colorful garb and have flowers in their hats. They carry a barrel of cheap beer and a keg of clear grain alcohol decorated with garlands of greenery which they set up on the table. Everyone drinks. Then they form a ring and dance and sing the risqué folk tune: "Two country girls." When that is finished they go out again singing.)

*

(JULIA *enters alone. She looks at the disorder in the kitchen and clasps her hands together; then she takes out a powder puff and powders her face.*)

JEAN. *(Enters; exalted)* There, you see! And you heard? Do you think we can stay here now?

JULIA. No I don't. But what are we to do?

JEAN. Run, travel, a long ways from here.

JULIA. Travel? Yes—but where?

JEAN. To Switzerland, the Italian lakes—have you ever been there?

JULIA. No! Is it beautiful there?

JEAN. Ahhh, everlasting summertime! Orange trees, laurels, ah!

JULIA. But what can we do down there?

JEAN. I'll start a hotel, with everything about it top-of-the-line and only first-class customers.

JULIA. Hotel?

JEAN. That's the life I tell you; constantly new faces, new languages. Never a minute's freedom to brood or worry; no searching for something to do—the work calls you: night and day the bells ring, the whistles blow, buses come and go. Always the clatter of gold coins on the counter. That's the life!

JULIA. Yes, that's a living. And me? *what will she do?*

JEAN. The mistress of the establishment; its chief ornament. With your looks . . . and your manners—oh it's a guaranteed success. Colossal! You'll sit like a queen at the counter and set the slaves in motion with the touch of an electric button. Guests will pass before your throne and timidly lay their tribute on your table. —You can't imagine how people tremble when they are presented with a bill— I'll salt the accounts and you'll spread sugar on them with your sweetest smiles. Oh, let's travel far from here *(Takes a timetable out of his pocket)* —Right away by the next train! We'll be in Malmo by 6:33; Hamburg by 8:40 tomorrow morning; Frankfurt—Basel in another day then to come by the Gotthard's line. Let me see: three days. Three days!

JULIA. That's all good. But, Jean—you must give me the nerve—tell me you love me! Come here and hold me!

JEAN. *(Hesitatingly)* I want to—but I don't dare. Not again in this house. I love you—no doubt of that—how can you doubt that, miss?

JULIA. *(Slyly, very womanly)* Miss?—Call me Julia! Between us there can be no more barriers. Call me Julia!

JEAN. *(Painfully)* I can't! There will be barriers between us always, as long as we remain in this house—here the past exists and here exists the Count—and I've never met another person I have so much respect for. I have only to catch sight of a pair of his gloves on a chair to feel small. I have only to hear that bell up there to jump like a skittish horse. Even now when I catch sight of his boots standing there so stiff and alert I want to bow. *(Kicking at the boots)* Superstition, custom, foisted upon you from the time you're a child—that means it must be possible to forget it. In another country, one that is a republic, men will bow to my liveried porters. Backs must be bent, understand, but not mine! I was not born for that, I'm made of sterner stuff—I have character—and if I only can get hold of the first branch, you'll see me climb! I'm a valet today, but next year I'll own a hotel. In ten years I'll retire; then I'll go to Rumania and buy a title. I could even—notice I say *could*—end up a count.

JULIA. Beautiful, beautiful!

JEAN. Ah, in Rumania you can buy a title. And so you'll become a countess after all! My countess!

JULIA. What do I care about all that now, I've thrown all that away! —Tell me you love me, otherwise—yes, otherwise what have I become?

JEAN. I'll tell you a thousand times—later. But not here! And above all don't get sentimental or everything is lost. We must look at it coldly, like sensible people *(Takes out a cigar, snips off the end and lights it)* Sit down over there! And I'll sit here, and we can talk as though nothing has happened.

JULIA. *(Despairingly)* Oh, my God! Have you no feelings?

JEAN. I? You won't find any man as deep feeling as I; but I know how to control myself also.

JULIA. A while ago you kissed my shoe—and now!

JEAN. *(Firmly)* Well, that was then! Now we have other things to think about.

JULIA. Don't speak to me so harshly!

JEAN. No, but sensibly. We've committed one mad act already, let's not commit any more. The Count could be here any moment and before that our fate must be settled. What do you think of my plan for the future? Do you approve?

JULIA. It seems all right on the whole, only one question: such a large undertaking will need a lot of money—Do you have that?

JEAN. *(Chewing his cigar)* I? Definitely! I have my knowledge of the profession, my wide experience, my skill with languages. That's the best capital there is, I must say.

JULIA. But with that you couldn't even buy a railroad ticket.

JEAN. You're right there; that's why I've been looking for a backer to advance the funds.

JULIA. Where'll you find him in such a hurry?

JEAN. That's up to you if you wish to be my partner!

JULIA. I can't do that, and I have nothing myself. *(Pause)*

JEAN. Then that falls through . . .

JULIA. And . . .

JEAN. Everything will be just as it was!

JULIA. Do you believe I'll stay under this roof as your whore? Do you really believe I'll let people point their fingers at me? Do you think I can look my father in the face after this? Never! Get me away from here, from humiliation and disgrace—Oh, what have I done? My God, my God! *(Crying)*

JEAN. So now we have come back to that again!—What have *you* done? The same as many before you.

JULIA. *(Sobbing uncontrollably)* And now you despise me! I'm falling, I'm falling!

JEAN. Then fall on me and I'll lift you up again!

JULIA. What terrible power dragged me to you? The weak drawn to the strong—the falling drawn to the rising? Or was it love? This is love? Do you even know what love is?

JEAN. I? Of course I do. Don't you believe I've been there before?

JULIA. Such words you use; such thoughts you think!

JEAN. As I was raised, so I am! Don't get nervous and start playing the fine lady; we're both in the same soup now. Look here, little girl, come let me offer you a glass of something extra special.

(He opens the drawer, and takes out the wine bottle and fills two used glasses.)

JULIA. Where did that wine come from?

JEAN. From the cellar.

JULIA. My father's burgundy!

JEAN. It'll do. For his son-in-law!

JULIA. And I drink beer!

JEAN. That only proves you have inferior taste to mine.

JULIA. Thief!

JEAN. Do you plan to tattle?

JULIA. Oh, oh! Accomplice to a house thief! Have I been drunk? Have I only been dreaming all night? Midsummer Night! The festival of innocent games . . .

irony

JEAN. Innocent—hmm!

JULIA. *(Pacing back and forth)* Could there be another human being on this earth at this moment as unhappy as I am!

JEAN. Why should you be? After such a conquest! Think of Kristine in there. Don't you think she has feelings also?

JULIA. I thought so a while ago, but not any longer! No, a peasant is a peasant . . .

JEAN. And a whore is a whore!

JULIA. *(On her knees with folded hands)* Oh God in Heaven, be done with this wretched life! Take me out of this filth I'm sinking into. Save me! Save me!

JEAN. I must admit I feel sorry for you. While I lay there in the onion patch and watched you in the rose garden well then . . . I can tell you now . . . I got the same nasty thoughts all boys get.

JULIA. Even you who wished to die for me!

JEAN. In the oat bin? That was all talk.

JULIA. Lies!

JEAN. *(Yawning sleepily)* Almost. There was a story I read in a paper about a chimney sweep who lay down in a wood box full of lilacs because he had been charged for the support of some brat . . .

JULIA. So that's what you're like . . .

JEAN. I had to hit on something. And I've found it always helps to really make a dandy show to catch a woman.

JULIA. Villain!

JEAN. *Merde!*

JULIA. And now you have seen the hawk's back . . .

JEAN. Well not exactly the *back* . . .

JULIA. And I was to be that first branch . . .

JEAN. But the branch was rotten . . .

JULIA. I was to be the signboard in front of the hotel . . .

JEAN. And I the hotel . . .

JULIA. Sit behind the counter, luring your customers, fixing your accounts . . .

JEAN. I'd do that myself . . .

JULIA. That a human soul can be so dipped in filth!

JEAN. Wash it then!

JULIA. Lackey, menial, stand up when I'm talking!

JEAN. Lackey's lay, menial's slut, shut your mouth and get out of here! Who the hell are you to call me filthy after the way you behaved here tonight? People of my class would never in their lives behave like that. Do you think any servant girl would throw herself at a man the way you did? Have you ever seen any girl of my class offer herself like that? I've seen it only among animals and prostitutes.

JULIA. *(Crushed)* That's right: hit me, step on me; I don't deserve any better. I'm vile; then help me! Help me out of this if there's a way to do it!

JEAN. *(More gently)* I'm not going to be low enough to deny my share of responsibility for what happened, but do

you think a person in my position would have dared look
up at you if you yourself hadn't offered the invitation? I'm
still astonished . . .

JULIA. And proud . . .

JEAN. Why shouldn't I be? Although I must admit the
conquest was so easy it gives me no great thrill.

JULIA. Strike me again!

JEAN. No! Forgive me for what I've been saying. I don't
believe in striking the helpless—least of all a woman. I can't
deny that it pleases me to find it was only fool's gold that
dazzled us down here; that the hawk is simply grey on the
back also; that there was powder covering the pale cheek,
and there's dirt under the polished nails; that a handkerchief may be soiled even though it smells of perfume . . . !
But it pains me to find that what I strived for is neither
higher nor more solidly based; to see you sink so low that
you are far beneath your own cook: that gives me the same
pain as seeing autumn flowers struck down by rain and
crumpled in the mud.

JULIA. How superior you sound.

JEAN. And I am! Can't you see I can transform you into
a countess, but you can never make me a count.

JULIA. But I am born of a count, and that's more than
you can ever accomplish!

JEAN. That's true: but I may become the father of
counts—if . . .

JULIA. And you are a thief: that I am not.

JEAN. Thief isn't the lowest. There's worse! But as for
that; when I serve in a house I think of myself as a member
of the family, like a child of the house, and you don't call
it stealing when children snitch a berry from loaded bushes.
(His passion is aroused again.) Miss Julia, you're a lovely
woman, far too good for the likes of me! You were intox-
icated, and now you want to cover your mistake by con-
vincing yourself that you're in love with me! But you aren't.
Unless that is what you call being tempted by my good
looks—in which case your love is no better than mine.—I
would never be satisfied knowing that you cared only for
the animal in me and that I could never win your true love.

JULIA. Do you mean that?

JEAN. Could it be possible?——Could I come to love you? Yes, no doubt of that! You are beautiful, you have class—*(Approaches her and takes hold of her hand)* educated, charming when you wish to be, and the man whose flame has been aroused by you will be battling an inferno. *(Puts his arm around her waist)* You're like a red-hot wine mulled with strong spices, and one kiss from you . . . *(He tries to lead her out; but she deftly slips out of his arms.)*

JULIA. Leave me be!—You can't win me like that!

JEAN. *How* then?—Not like that! Not by caresses and sweet talk; not by planning the future, nor escape from disgrace! *How* then?

JULIA. How? How? I've no idea—None at all!—I abhor you the same way I abhor rats, but I can't get away from you!

JEAN. Get away with me!

JULIA. *(Straightening herself up)* Get away? Yes, we will get away!—But I'm so tired. Give me a glass of wine.

(JEAN pours the wine.)

JULIA. *(Looks at her watch)* We must talk first. We still have a little time. *(Drinks her glass down and holds it out for more)*

JEAN. Don't drink so much. You'll get drunk!

JULIA. What's the difference?

JEAN. Difference? It's vulgar to get drunk!—Well, what do you have to say?

JULIA. We have to get away. But first let's talk it over. I need that because you've done all the talking so far. You've told me your life story, now I have to tell you mine. That way we'll know each other right to the bottom before we set out on this journey together.

JEAN. One moment! Beg pardon, but think it over. You may regret giving away the prize of your life's secrets.

JULIA. Aren't you my friend?

JEAN. Yes, sometimes—but don't count on it.

JULIA. That's just your way of talking.—And besides, my secrets are known by everyone.—You see my mother was of common birth, really lowly stock. She had been brought up with the notions of the times about equality, women's rights and all that. And she was dead set against marriage. Therefore when my father proposed to her she swore she would never be his wife, but . . . then she did anyway. I came into this world—against my mother's will I've come to believe. My mother decided to bring me up in a perfectly natural state and to teach me everything that a boy should learn, in order to set an example that a woman could be as good as a man. I went around in boys' clothes, and was taught to handle horses and had nothing to do with the cows.° I had to groom, put on harness and even hunt, riding astride. Then I was forced to learn farming! And all over the estate men did women's jobs and women did the men's—with the result that the whole place fell apart, and we became the laughing stock of the countryside. Eventually my father woke up from the spell he was under and he rebelled, so everything was changed around again. My mother became ill—what kind of illness I don't know—but she often had cramps and she hid away in the attic or in the garden, and sometimes she stayed out all night. Then came the big fire you've heard about. The house, the stable, and the barn burned down. Circumstances seemed to indicate arson, and the unlucky event occurred the day after the insurance had expired because my father's payment had been delayed by a careless messenger. *(She fills her glass and drinks.)*

JEAN. Don't drink any more!

JULIA. Oh, what does that matter!—We had only the clothes on our backs and had to sleep in the carriages. My father didn't know where he could get the money to rebuild the house. Then my mother suggested that he seek a loan from a childhood friend of hers, a brickmaker in the vicinity. Father got the loan, but was not required to pay any interest, which astonished him. And so the estate was

°In Scandinavia cattle and gardening were women's responsibilities.

built up again. *(Drinks again)* Do you know who set fire to the estate?

JEAN. Her ladyship, your mother!

JULIA. Do you know who the brickmaker was?

JEAN. Your mother's lover?

JULIA. Do you know whose money it was?

JEAN. Just a minute—No, I don't know that.

JULIA. It was my mother's!

JEAN. Also the Count's, unless there was a marriage agreement.

JULIA. There was no agreement. My mother had a modest fund which she did not wish to have come into my father's control, therefore she had invested it with her—friend.

JEAN. Who tricked them!

JULIA. Precisely! He kept it!—My father found it all out. He couldn't sue; he couldn't pay off his wife's lover, nor prove that it was his wife's money! —That was how my mother took revenge because he had taken control of his household.—That's when he came close to shooting himself—it was even said that he had tried and missed! But he survived, and my mother was made to suffer for her handiwork! Those were five years I'll never forget! I sympathized with my father but sided with my mother because I didn't know all the circumstances. From her I learned to mistrust and hate all men—because she hated anything masculine—and I swore to her that I would never be any man's slave.

JEAN. But you became engaged to the Royal Commissioner.

JULIA. I only did that so he would become my slave.

JEAN. And he wouldn't?

JULIA. He would have, but I wouldn't let him! I grew tired of him!

JEAN. I saw that—in the stable yard.

JULIA. What did you see?

JEAN. What you said—how he broke off the engagement.

JULIA. That's a lie! I was the one who broke it off! Did he say he did it, the villain?

JEAN. Not exactly a villain. So you hate all men, My Lady?

JULIA. Yes!—Most of the time!. But now and then—when my weakness comes on, oh God!

JEAN. You hate me also?

JULIA. Absolutely! I would like to kill you like some wild animal . . .

JEAN. As one doesn't hesitate to shoot a mad dog. Right?

JULIA. Yes!

JEAN. But now you can't find anything to shoot with—and there is no dog! What are we to do?

JULIA. Travel!

JEAN. To torment each other to death!

JULIA. No—to enjoy two days, eight days, as long as possible, and then—to die . . .

JEAN. Die? That's stupid! I think it's better to set up a hotel!

JULIA. *(Without hearing JEAN)*—at Lake Como, where the sun always shines, where laurel trees are green as Yuletide and oranges glow.

JEAN. Lake Como is a rain hole and I never saw an orange there except in the vegetable market; but it is a good place for tourists because there are a lot of cottages there to rent to lovers, and that's a very profitable industry— Do you know why—? Well, they take a lease for six months—and then they leave after three weeks!

JULIA. *(Naively)* Why after three weeks?

JEAN. Because they quarrel, of course. But the rent still has to be paid! And so you rent the house again. And it goes on that way all the time because there's always a supply of love—even if it doesn't last long.

JULIA. You don't want to die with me?

JEAN. I don't want to die at all. I'm too fond of living, and I regard suicide to be a great sin against the One who gave us life.

JULIA. You believe in God,—*you?*

JEAN. Of course I do! And I go to church every other Sunday. —Now, to put in bluntly, I've grown tired of all this and I'm going to bed.

JULIA. Oh yes, and you think I'll be satisfied with that? Don't you think a man owes something to a woman he has dishonored?

JEAN. *(Takes out his purse and throws a silver coin on the table)* Please yourself! I don't want to be in debt to anyone.

JULIA. *(Without taking notice of the insult)* You know what the law provides—

JEAN. It's unfortunate that the law provides no punishment for a woman who seduces a man.

JULIA. Can you think of any way out except that we go abroad, marry and then divorce?

JEAN. And if I refuse to enter into such a *Mésalliance?*

JULIA. *Mésalliance* . . .

JEAN. Yes, for me. You see I have a better ancestry than you, there is no arson in my family.

JULIA. Can you be sure?

JEAN. Nothing to the contrary is known, for we record no pedigree—except with the police! But I've traced your pedigree in a book on the drawing-room table. Do you know who your first ancestor was? It was a miller who let his wife sleep with the king one night during the Danish war. I don't have any ancestor like that, but I can become an ancestor myself!

JULIA. That's what I get for opening my heart to one so unworthy, for that I threw away my family's honor . . .

JEAN. Dishonor!—Well see, I told you so! One should not drink for then one talks. And one *must* not talk!

JULIA. Oh, how I regret it!—How I regret it!—If only you loved me!

JEAN. For the last time: What do you mean by that? Should I weep; should I hop over your riding crop; should I kiss you, lure you down to Lake Como for three weeks, and so on . . . What am I to do? What do you expect? It's beginning to become a pain! But that's what you get when you stick your nose into women's affairs. Lady Julia! I see that you are unhappy; I know you are suffering; but I can't understand your kind. You won't see us make that kind of a fuss; there is no such hatred among us. We love like we play, when our work allows us the time; but we don't have time to do it all night and day as you do! I believe you're sick; I'm certain that you're sick.

JULIA. Just be kind to me and talk to me like a human being.

JEAN. Then act human yourself! You spit on me and refuse to let me wipe it off—on you!

JULIA. Help me, help me! Tell me what I am to do—where I can turn.

JEAN. Jesus Christ, if I only knew myself!

JULIA. I've been infuriating, I've been crazy, but there must be some way I can be saved.

JEAN. Stay here and keep quiet. No one knows a thing.

JULIA. Impossible! Those peasants know and Kristine knows!

JEAN. They don't know, and they would never believe it was possible.

JULIA. *(Hesitatingly)* But—It could happen again!

JEAN. That's true.

JULIA. And consequently?

JEAN. *(Frightened)* Consequences!—Where was my head when I didn't think of that! Yes, well only one thing—go away! At once! I can't go along, then everything would be lost, so you must travel alone—abroad—just anywhere!

JULIA. Alone? Where?—I can't!

JEAN. You must! And before the Count returns. Stay and you know what will come of that! One little slip-up and you want to go on doing it; after all, the harm's already been done . . . You get bolder and bolder and—at last it all comes out! You must go away! Then write to the Count and tell him everything, except that it was me. He'll never guess! And I don't think he'll be anxious to find that out!

JULIA. I'll go if you come with me!

JEAN. Are you crazy, woman? Lady Julia to run away with her father's valet! It would be in the papers in the morning and the Count would never live through it.

JULIA. I can't go! I can't stay here! Help me! I'm so tired, so dreadfully tired. —Order me! Set me in motion. I can't think, can't act by myself . . . !

JEAN. You people are phonies. You puff yourselves up and turn up your noses as though you were the Lords of creation! Well, I will give you orders! Go up and change clothes; get some travel money and come back here!

JULIA. *(Softly)* Come up with me!

JEAN. To your room?—Now you're crazy again! *(He hesitates a moment.)* No! Go, at once! *(Takes her hand and leads her out)*

JULIA. (As she exits) Try to say it kindly, Jean!

JEAN. An order always sounds unkind. You'd better learn that!

(JEAN is now alone. He draws a sigh of relief, sits down at the table, takes out a notebook and pencil, adds some figures, sometimes out loud. He works for a time until KRISTINE enters dressed for church. She carries a formal shirt and a white tie.)

KRISTINE. Lord Jesus, how this place looks! What have you been up to?

JEAN. Oh, the young lady dragged everyone in here. You slept so hard you didn't hear anything.

KRISTINE. Like a log.

JEAN. And already dressed for church?

KRISTINE. Ye-es! Didn't you promise to come with me to communion today?

JEAN. Yes, I did!—And you've got the gear! Well, come then! *(Sits down; KRISTINE helps dress him in the formal shirt and white tie. There is a pause.)*

JEAN. *(Sleepily)* What's the text today?

KRISTINE. It'll be about John the Baptist losing his head, I suppose!

JEAN. It takes a long time to tell that—Aye, you're choking me!—Oh, I'm sleepy, so-o-o sleepy.

KRISTINE. Well, what kept you up all night? You're almost green in the face!

JEAN. I sat here talking with Miss Julia.

KRISTINE. She hasn't the least idea what's proper, that one!

(Another pause)

JEAN. Kristine, dear, are you listening?

KRISTINE. We-e-ll?

JEAN. It's really funny when you think about it—Her!

KRISTINE. What's so funny?

JEAN. Everything.

(Pause)

KRISTINE. *(Catches sight of the glasses on the table, one only half empty)* So you drank together also?

JEAN. Yes.

KRISTINE. Shame!—Look into my eyes!

JEAN. Yes!

KRISTINE. *Is* it possible? *Is* it possible?

JEAN. *(After a moment's thought)* Yes! It is!

KRISTINE. Ugh! That's far worse than I could've believed. No! Shame, shame!

JEAN. You aren't jealous of her are you?

KRISTINE. No, not of her. If it had been Clara or Sophie I'd have scratched out your eyes.—Yes, that's how I feel and I can't say why. —It was a shameful thing to do!

JEAN. You're mad at her then?

KRISTINE. No,—at you! It was wrong to do it, very wrong! Poor girl! —No, I tell you, I won't stay in this house any longer; where I can't possibly feel respect for my employers.

JEAN. Why is it necessary to feel respect for them?

KRISTINE. You ask that, and you think you're so smart? One should never serve people who cannot behave decently—Right? I think that only degrades you.

JEAN. Yes, but it is comforting to know they aren't any better than we are.

KRISTINE. I won't accept that. If they're no better then what's the use of trying to become better people. —And think of the Count! Think of him. He's had so much sadness in his days! No, I can't stay in this house anymore!— And with the likes of you! If it had been the royal commissioner, someone from her own class . . .

JEAN. Why that dig?

KRISTINE. Well, yes! You're all right in your way, but there's some difference between people all the same. —No,

I can't forget how proud the mistress was, so critical of menfolk that you'd think she'd never let one come near her—and one like you! She wanted poor Diana shot for running loose with the gatekeeper's dog! —Well, I do say! —No, I won't stay here any longer! By October twenty-fourth I'll be on my way.

JEAN. And then?

KRISTINE. Well, since we've come around to that, per-haps it's time you looked for something also, since we're planning to get married.

JEAN. Yes, then what am I to look for? I won't find as good a place as this if I'm married.

KRISTINE. No, I understand that! But you could work as a janitor or maybe a doorkeeper or some such. Civil service is cheap but it's steady, and then the widow and children get a pension—

prestige

JEAN. *(With a grimace)* That's all very well and good but it's hardly my style to plan to up and die for wife and children. I must say I was looking forward to something a bit loftier.

KRISTINE. Your plans, yes! But you have obligations also! Remember that, man!

JEAN. Don't get me riled up with talk of obligations! Any-way I know what I've got to do! *(Listening outside)* We've plenty of time to mull this over. Go in now and get ready and then we'll go to church.

KRISTINE. Who's that walking around up there?

JEAN. I don't know, unless it's Clara.

KRISTINE. It couldn't be the Count already, come home without anyone hearing him?

JEAN. *(Frightened)* The Count? No, that's not possible. I didn't hear the bell.

KRISTINE. *(Exiting)* God help us! I've never seen the likes!

(The sun has risen and shines on the treetops out in the estate grounds. The light changes little-by-little till it slants in through the windows.)

JULIA. *(Enters in travelling clothes carrying a little bird-cage covered with a hand towel. She places it on a chair.*

She is extremely nervous, and it is evident when she speaks.)
I'm ready now.

JEAN. Shh! Kristine is awake!

JULIA. Does she suspect anything?

JEAN. She doesn't know anything! But, my God, look at you!

JULIA. What?

JEAN. You're as pale as a corpse and—forgive me but your face is smudged.

JULIA. Let me wash it then—now! *(She crosses to the washstand and washes her face and hands.)* Give me a towel!— Oh, that's the sun coming up!

JEAN. And then the trolls explode.

JULIA. Yes, there were trolls and evil spirits out last night! —But, Jean, come with me! I've got the means now!

JEAN. *(Doubtfully)* Enough?

JULIA. Enough for a start. Come with me, I can't travel alone today. Imagine, Midsummer Day, a stuffy train packed with masses of people who stare at you; standing still at stations when you want to race. No, I can't, I can't! Then the memories come; childhood memories of Midsummer Days when they adorned the church with branches of birch and lilac, dinners at the loaded table, relatives, friends; afternoons out on the lawns, dancing, music, flowers, and games! Oh, one can run, run away, but memories go with you in the baggage car, and remorse, and repentance!

JEAN. I'll go with you—but at once, before it's too late. This very instant!

JULIA. Then get ready. *(Picks up the birdcage)*

JEAN. No baggage! That would give us away.

JULIA. No, not a thing! Only what we can take in the car.

JEAN. *(Has his hat)* What have you got? What is that?

JULIA. Only my finch. I can't leave it behind.

JEAN. Now I've seen it all! Taking a birdcage along! You really are crazy. Drop it!

JULIA. It's all I'm taking with me from my home; The only living thing that cares for me since Diana deserted me! Don't be cruel! Just let me take it along!

JEAN. Drop the cage, I say!—And don't talk so loud—
Kristine will hear us.

JULIA. No, I won't let it fall into the hands of strangers.
I'd rather you killed it!

JEAN. Well give it here, and I'll wring its neck!

JULIA. Yes, but don't hurt it! Don't . . . no, I can't!

JEAN. Let me; I can!

JULIA. *(Takes the bird out of the cage and kisses it)* Oh,
my little Serina, must you die and leave your mistress!

JEAN. Please don't make a scene; you know it's a matter
of your life, of your future? Well, quickly! *(Grabs the bird
from her, takes it to the chopping block and picks up the
butcher knife;* MISS JULIA *turns her back.)* You should have
been taught to kill chickens instead of firing a revolver—
(Chops the bird's head) then you wouldn't faint at a drop
of blood.

JULIA. *(Shrieking)* Kill me also! Kill me! If you can
butcher an innocent animal without a trembling hand. Oh,
I hate and despise you; there is blood between us! I curse
the moment I met you, I curse the moment my mother
conceived me!

JEAN. Well, what help is all that cursing? Come on!

JULIA. *(Approaching the chopping block as though drawn
to it against her will)* No, I don't want to go yet; I can't
. . . I must see . . . Hush! I hear a carriage coming—*(She
listens without taking her eyes from the block and the knife.)*
You think I can't bear the sight of blood! You think I am
so weak . . . Oh—I would like to see your blood, your brains
on that block—I would like to see everyone of the male
sex swimming in a sea of blood . . . I think I'd be able to
drink out of your skull, I could bathe my feet in your open
breast and eat your heart roasted whole! —You think I am
weak; you think I love you because the fruit of my womb
yearns for seed; you think I wish to bear your offspring
under my heart and nourish it with my blood—give birth
to your children and take your name! Tell me, what are
you called? I've never heard your last name—could it be
you don't have one? Shall I become Mrs. "Woodshed"—

or Madame "Slopbucket"—you dog who wears my collar;
you lackey who bears my coat of arms on your buttons—
I'm to share you with my cook, be a rival to my maid. Oh!
Oh! Oh! —You think I'm a coward and want to run away!
No, I'm going to stay—and let the lightning strike. My
father comes home—finds his desk broken open—his
money stolen! Then he'll ring—on the bell . . . two times
for the valet— and then I'll tell everything! Everything!
Oh, it will be good to have an end to it—if only that can
be the end! —And so his heart breaks and he dies! . . . That
puts an end to all of us—and then there is silence . . . peace!
. . . eternal rest!— Like the family crest on the coffin—the
Count's line is wiped out—and the valet's descendants
carry it on in an orphanage . . . winning laurels in the gutter
and ending in a jail.

JEAN. That was royal blood talking! Bravo, Lady Julia!
Put the miller back in the sack!

(KRISTINE *enters dressed for church with her psalm book
in her hand.*)

JULIA. (*Rushes to her and throws herself in her arms as
though for protection*) Help me, Kristine! Help me against
this man!

KRISTINE. (*Unmoved and cold*) What kind of spectacle is
this on a Sabbath morning? (*Sees the chopping block*) And
such a mess you've made—What's this all about? And all
this shrieking and carrying on?

JULIA. Kristine! You're a woman and you're my friend!
Don't go near that villain!

JEAN. (*A little shy and embarrassed*) While the ladies are
talking, I'll go and shave. (*Slips out to the right*)

JULIA. I want you to understand. —Listen to me!

KRISTINE. I can't make sense of these cheap goings-on.
Where are you off to in your travelling clothes—and him
with his hat on— well? —Well?

JULIA. Listen, Kristine; just listen and I'll tell you everything—

KRISTINE. I don't want to know anything . . .

JULIA. You must listen to me . . .

KRISTINE. About what? Is it this nonsense with Jean? Well, I don't care anything about that: it's none of my business. But if you're thinking of taking him away with you, we'll put a stop to that!

JULIA. *(Extremely nervous now)* Please try to be calm Kristine, and listen to me. I can't stay here, and Jean can't stay here—we simply must get away . . .

KRISTINE. Hm, hm!

JULIA. *(Brightening)* But look, I have an idea. —Suppose all three of us go. —Abroad —to Switzerland and set up a hotel together, —I have money, you see— and Jean and I can run the place—and you, I was thinking, could run the kitchen . . . Isn't that great! —Say yes, now! And come with us, then everything is arranged! —Say yes! Do! *(Hugs KRIS-TINE and pats her)*

KRISTINE. *(Coldly and thoughtfully)* Hm, hm!

JULIA. *(Fast tempo)* You never got to travel, Kristine— You should get out and have a look at the world. You can't imagine the fun of travelling by train—new people all the time—new lands—and then we go to the theatres and attend the opera—and then we'll get to Munich, where, you know, they have lots of museums, and they have Rubens and Raphael and all those great painters you know about— You must have heard stories about Munich, where King Ludwig lived—the king, you know, who went mad?—And we can see his castle—he still has some castles furnished just like in the fairy tales—and from there it isn't far to Switzerland—and the Alps, you know— Just imagine the Alps with snow on them in the summer—and there are oranges and laurel trees that are green all year round,—

(JEAN is seen to the right, sharpening his razor on a strop which he holds between his teeth and his left hand. He is listening to the speech with a pleased expression and nods his approval from time to time.)

JULIA. *(Still faster tempo)* And then we'll buy a hotel!— And I'll sit at the counter while Jean stands out and greets the tourists . . . and does the shopping . . . writes letters— That'll be the life, mind you—there's the train whistle, there's the arriving buses, there's ringing from the rooms, there's ringing in the restaurant—and I'll make out all the bills—I'm going to pad them all, I am . . . You can hardly imagine how timid tourists are when they come to pay their accounts! —And you—you'll sit like a queen in the kitchen. —Naturally you won't stand at the stove yourself—and you'll always be neatly and nicely dressed in order to show yourself to people—and with your looks— Yes, I'm not flattering you now—you'll catch a husband one fine day! A rich Englishman, you know—those fellows are so easy to—*(Beginning to slow down)*—to trap. —And so we'll get rich—and build ourselves a villa on Lake Como.— Of course it rains there occasionally—but—*(Sluggishly)* the sun has to shine some of the time. —Although it looks dark out—and—then—or else we can come home again—and come back—*(Pause)*—here—or some other place—

KRISTINE.   Now you just listen to me. Do you really believe all that yourself, miss?

JULIA.   *(Completely crushed)* Do I believe it myself?

KRISTINE.   Yes!

JULIA.   *(Exhausted)* I don't know; I don't believe anything anymore. *(She sinks onto a bench, laying her head between her arms on the table.)* Nothing! Nothing at all!

KRISTINE.   *(Turns to right where* JEAN *is standing)* Un huh! He thought he'd run away!

JEAN.   *(Crestfallen, sets the razor down on the table)* Run away? Well that's a bit strong! You've heard what the young lady proposes, and although she's tired from being up all night, it is a proposal that could be carried out very well!

KRISTINE.   Now you listen to me! Did you think I would act as cook for that one there . . .

JEAN.   *(Sharply)* Please use proper language when you speak to your mistress!

KRISTINE.   Mistress!?

JEAN.   Yes!

KRISTINE.   Well, now! Listen to that!

JEAN. Yes, it would do you good to listen more and talk less! Miss Julia is your mistress and lack of respect to her now is the same as lack of respect for yourself!

KRISTINE. I've always had enough respect for myself—

JEAN. —So none's left for others!

KRISTINE. —So I don't stoop below my station. Nobody can say that the Count's cook has had anything to do with the stable hand or the swineherd! Nobody can say that!

JEAN. Yes, you've only had to do with a gentleman, that was your luck!

KRISTINE. Yes, it's a fine gentleman who sells the Count's oats out of the stable—

JEAN. You should talk, you who gets a commission on the groceries and takes bribes from the butcher.

KRISTINE. What's that?

JEAN. And so you have no respect for your gentry any longer! You, you, you!

KRISTINE. Are you coming with me to church? You could use a good sermon after such exploits!

JEAN. No, I'm not going to church today; you can go by yourself and confess your own deeds.

KRISTINE. Yes, that I'll do. And I'll bring home enough forgiveness to cover you also! The Savior suffered and died on the cross for all our sins, and whoever shall go to him with a true and repentant heart, so taketh he all your sins upon himself.

JEAN. Even from those most steeped in sin?

JULIA. Do you believe that, Kristine?

KRISTINE. It's my living faith, as sure as I stand here, and it is my childhood belief which I have kept since I was young, Miss Julia. And where sin abounds, there grace and mercy abound!

JULIA. Oh if I had your faith! Oh, if only . . .

KRISTINE. Yes, but you see, one can't have it without God's special grace, and that is not bestowed on everyone—

JULIA. Who is it bestowed on?

KRISTINE. That's the very secret of the workings of grace, your Ladyship, and God has no regard to persons, but those that are the last shall be the first . . .

JULIA. Yes, but doesn't that mean he has regard for those who stand last?

KRISTINE. *(Continuing)*—and it is easier for a camel to pass through the eye of a needle than for a rich man to come into God's presence! You see, that's how it is, Miss Julia! No, I'm going however—alone, and in passing I'll tell the stable man not to let out any of the horses, in case anyone should like to get away before the Count comes home!—Goodbye! *(She exits.)*

JEAN. What a she-devil!—And all for the sake of a pet bird!—

JULIA. *(Dully)* Forget the finch!—Can't you see a way out of this, to put an end to it?

JEAN. *(Thinking deeply)* No!

JULIA. What would you do in my place?

JEAN. In yours? What to do?—as one wellborn—a woman, who has—fallen. I don't know—yes! I do know!

JULIA. *(Picks up the razor and makes a meaningful gesture)* Like this?

JEAN. Yes!—But *I* wouldn't do that—mark that! There is a difference between us!

JULIA. Because you are a man and I am a woman? What is the difference?

JEAN. There is a difference—between male and female!

JULIA. *(With the razor in her hand)* I want to! But I can't!—My father couldn't either, when the proper time came.

JEAN. It was not the proper time for him! First he had to get revenge!

JULIA. And now it is my mother's turn for revenge—through me.

JEAN. Didn't you ever love your father, Miss Julia?

JULIA. Yes, boundlessly, but I must have hated him at the same time! I must have done that without realizing it! But he was the one who brought me up to despise my own sex, till I was half woman, half man! Who is at fault for what has happened? My father, my mother, myself! My self? There's nothing to my self! I haven't a single thought

men = intelligent – rational
women = emotional – not rational

She won't let Jesus take guilt

that didn't come to me from my father; no single passion
that didn't come from my mother; and now this stuff about
all human beings being equal—I got that from him, my
fiancé—and for that I hate him! How can it be my own
fault? Transfer my guilt to Jesus, as Kristine does?—No,
I'm too proud to do that. —And too smart—thanks to my
father's teaching. —And that about the rich man not getting
into Heaven, that's a lie, and Kristine, who has money in
the savings bank, couldn't get in anyhow! Whose fault is
it? What does it matter whose it is! For I'm the one no
matter who must bear the guilt, bear the consequences . . .

JEAN. Yes, but—

*(The bell gives two sharp rings. MISS JULIA jumps to her
feet. JEAN changes his coat.)*

JEAN. The Count is home! Think, if Kristine—*(Goes to
the speaking tube; knocks on it and listens)*

JULIA. Has he been to his desk?

JEAN. This is Jean, your Lordship! *(He listens. Note: the
audience should not hear what the COUNT says.)* Yes, your
Lordship! *(Listening again)* Yes, your Lordship! At once!
(Listening again) Soon, your Lordship! *(Listening)* Un huh!
In half an hour!

JULIA. *(Greatly concerned)* What did he say? Lord Jesus,
what did he say?

JEAN. He ordered his boots and wants his coffee in half
an hour.

JULIA. Only half hour then. Oh, I'm so tired; I can't
do anything, I can't repent, can't run away, or stay, can't
live—or die! Help me now! Command me, and I'll obey
like a dog! Do me this last favor; save my honor, save his
name! You know what I *must* do, but my will is weak . . .
You must will it, and make me do it!

she is paralyzed

JEAN. I don't know why—but now I can't either—I don't
understand—It's as if this coat here made a—I can't give
orders to you—and now since the Count spoke to me—
now—I can't rightly explain it—but—oh, the damned servant is back in my spine!—I believe if the Count were to
come down here now—and order me to cut my throat, I'd
do it on the spot.

born into social position - can't change

JULIA. Pretend that you are he, and I am you. You did some great acting on your knees before me—then you were nobility.—Or else—have you ever seen a hypnotist?

(JEAN nods assent.)

JULIA. He says to his subject: Grasp the broom. The man grasps it. He says: sweep! And the man sweeps—

JEAN. But then the other must be sleeping.

JULIA. *(Ecstatically)* I'm sleeping already—the whole room seems full of smoke to me . . . and you look like some kind of iron stove . . . that only resembles a man in a black coat and high hat—and your eyes glow like coals when the fire is going out—and your face is a pile of white ashes— *(The sunlight falls in on the floor now, and its beams light JEAN.)* —It is so warm and good— *(She rubs her hands as though to warm them before a fire.)* —And so bright—and so pleasant!

JEAN. *(Takes the razor and puts it in her hand)* There is the broom! Go now while it is light—to the barn—and . . . *(Whispers in her ear)*

JULIA. *(Wakening)* Thanks! Now I can rest! But before I go tell me—that the first also may receive the gift of grace. Say it, even if you don't believe it.

JEAN. The first? No, I can't say that!—But wait—Miss Julia—remember this! You no longer stand among the foremost—now you are among the—lowest!

JULIA. That's right. I am among the lowest, I am the least of all! Oh!—but I've lost the will again—tell me again that I must go!

JEAN. No, now I can't either! I cannot!

JULIA. And they that are the foremost shall be last!

JEAN. Don't think, don't think! Why are you taking away my strength also, so that I become a coward— What? I thought I saw the bell move! —No! It was the pattern on the wall!—To be so afraid of a bell! —Yes, but that isn't only a bell—there is someone behind it—a hand sets it in motion—and something else makes the hand move—but if you only cover your ears—cover your ears! Yes, now it rings even worse! Rings again until you answer—and then it is too late! And then the sheriff comes—and then— *(Two sharp rings of the bell. JEAN shrinks together; then he straightens himself up.)* It's terrible! But there's no other possible end!—Go!

(Miss Julia exits firmly through the door.)

decisive

bibliography

Henrik Ibsen

Downs, Brian. *Ibsen: The Intellectual Background.* 1946.
Ibsen, Henrik. *Letters and Speeches*, ed. by Evert Spinchorn. 1964.
Koht, Halvdan. *The Life of Ibsen.* 1931.
Meyer, Michael. *Ibsen: A Biography.* 1971.
Northam, John. *Ibsen's Dramatic Method.* 1953.
Shaw, G. Bernard. *The Quintessence of Ibsenism.* 1913.
Tennant, P. F. *Ibsen's Dramatic Technique.* 1948.
Weigand, Hermann. *The Modern Ibsen.* 1925.

August Strindberg

Dahlstrom, C. E. W. L. *Strindberg's Dramatic Expressionism.* 1930.
McGill, V. J. *August Strindberg: The Bedeviled Viking.* 1930.
Meyer, Michael. *Strindberg: A Biography.* 1985.
Mortenson, Brita, and Brian Downs. *Strindberg.* 1949.
Strindberg, August. *Open Letters to the Intimate Theater.* 1955.

General

Bentley, Eric. *The Playwright as Thinker.* 1946.
Brockett, Oscar G., and Robert R. Findlay. *Century of Innovation.* 1973.
Lucas, F. L. *The Drama of Ibsen and Strindberg.* 1962.
Valency, Maurice. *The Flower and the Castle.* 1963.
Williams, Raymond. *Drama from Ibsen to Eliot.* 1952.

Other writings by the two playwrights are also available; they include Ibsen's notebooks and letters and speeches, and Strindberg's copious diaries and open letters and forewords.